How to Hunt Birds with Gun Dogs

How to Hunt Birds with Gun Dogs

Bill Tarrant

STACKPOLE
BOOKS

Published by
STACKPOLE BOOKS
5067 Ritter Road
Mechanicsburg, PA 17055

Printed in the United States of America

First Edition

10 9 8 7 6 5 4 3 2

Also by Bill Tarrant
Best Way to Train Your Gun Dog
Bill Tarrant's Gun Dog Book: A Treasury of Happy Tails
Hey Pup, Fetch It Up!: The Complete Retriever Training Book
Problem Gun Dogs
Tarrant Trains Gun Dogs
Training the Hunting Retriever: The New Approach

Library of Congress Cataloging-in-Publication Data

Tarrant, Bill.
    How to hunt birds with gun dogs / Bill Tarrant. – 1st ed.
       p.   cm.
    Includes index.
    ISBN 0-8117-0845-4
    1. Fowling. 2. Bird dogs. I. Title.
  SK313.T37   1994
  799.24 – dc20   94-10039
                                                    CIP

Portions of this book first appeared in *Field & Stream,* copyright 1986, 1987, 1993 by Times Mirror Magazines Inc.

All photographs by Bill Tarrant unless otherwise noted

THIS BOOK IS dedicated to every bird hunter who ever ripped out the crotch of his pants caught astraddle a five-strand barbed-wire fence; took a gun dog into a motel room after the day's hunt and awakened — fumigatingly stunned — when it was discovered, overnight, that your buddy for life had the drizzles; plunged into a nutria hole while wading to a duck blind in the Mississippi delta; walked across a cottonfield to go dove hunting and stepped on a rattlesnake; leaped from a pit blind and ran across a stubblefield yelling at a guy in a truck who left the road and stole the goose you'd just shot; finally found prairie chickens on top a knoll after hunting all day and fired the over-and-under to have it double barrel and knock you over backwards; carefully aimed and fired at the only mallard drake to come in all day and have the shot erupt in feathers. (Your buddy stayed up all night cramming that plumage into an empty shell casing and sneaked it into your shotgun so he could yell, "My God, you undressed him and he's flying away.") And you've shot into the wind, and all the exploded feathers are settling down on your arms and hat and shoulders; you cannot help but laugh, though you really want to kill the guy and bury him beneath the blind.

To have done these things, *or ever had a hankering to see men so discombobulated,* this is the book for you. But tell me first, how did you get out of that motel room without paying for a new carpet?

Contents

Foreword   xi

Acknowledgments   xiii

Introduction   1

1   *The Great American Bird Hunting Expedition*   8

2   *The Ring-necked Pheasant*   26

3   *Bobwhite Quail*   44

4   *Gambel's Quail*   65

5   *Mearns Quail*   72

6   *Scaled Quail*   80

7   *California Quail*   87

8   *Mountain Quail*   91

9   *Chukar*   96

10   *Sage Hen*   101

11   *Blue Grouse*   107

12   *Ruffed Grouse and Woodcock*   113

13   *Doves and Pigeons*   121

14   *Prairie Chickens*   127

15   *Sharptail Grouse and Hungarian Partridge*   134

16   *Puddle Ducks*   143

17   *Divers, Geese, and Brant*   156

Index   171

Foreword

BILL TARRANT IS the top gun dog writer in America today. When he writes a gun dog book you can take it to the bank. It's good as gold. Or more to the point, you can take it to the bird field, for you're going to get into birds.

I know of no other man who has hunted more countries for more different kinds of birds with more breeds of gun dogs than Bill. It's been his life's love and his life's work.

Rarely do you find a man who can do two things well. But that's Bill. No one has worked out a better training program for gun dogs or has more savvy in taking man and dog alike bird hunting. And no one but Bill has the ability to write about it so a man enjoys reading what he says as well as learning something.

Bill was the first man named Writer of the Year by the Dog Writers Association of America, and the only dog writer to ever write the story of the year – in all media – as judged by the Outdoor Writers Association of America. Each month he speaks to 14,400,000 outdoorsmen from the pages of *Field & Stream*, and has for twenty-two years.

There are a ton of books out there to tell you how to train a bird dog and how to take him hunting, but until you read this book you ain't read none at all.

Hoyle Eaton
Booneville, Mississippi
Winner: Four National Bird Dog Championships
Member: Field Trial Hall of Fame

Acknowledgments

IN MY WRITING studio I have a covey of cuties on staff—seven female assistants—who among other things:

Bust me out of writer's block by frolicking on my lap;

Soothe me with the warmth of their bodies when quail call in the hollow and deadlines will not let me slip away;

Kiss my cheek when the computer eats two chapters;

And cuddle with me in the La-Z-Boy as daylight approaches and the fingers can type no more.

Therefore, I reward these gals for their endless years of devotion, love, and affection.

They are Muffy, Sugar, Candy, Chili, Tiffy, Puddin, and Punk.

Six Lhasa Apsos and a Westie

Who in all their lives have never been more than a whistle away.

Introduction

THIS IS A gunpowder-smoked, mud-clad, lifetime-proven, bird-hunter's help book. A hands-on, frayed-cuff, gun-stock-scarred-and-bluing-rubbed-off, no-nonsense book about hunting, gun dogs, and North American gamebirds.

Read this book and you'll get your dog into birds and birds in your bag. Read this book and your kids will figure any meat on the table that ain't got shot in it is not fit to eat, for it's a road kill. Read this book and you'll have earned pride, and yes, joy, to last the rest of your life. For you'll be doing what God put you on earth to do, with a dog He built just special for the job.

But don't think this book will further any game-hog notion that if they fly they die. Just the opposite. In this book we harvest only what we eat. And we don't necessarily shoot for the limit.

As a young man I left the arena of man and holed up on a bit of land with an 18-acre pond. I hung my waders in the mud room, built a holding kennel just outside the door (in which I put two retrievers brought across the creek each night from the main kennel), and bought an automatic coffee pot with a timer so the brew would be ready as I reached the kitchen.

Then the alarm would ring, I'd pull on wool socks, head down the stairs, fill my thermos with coffee, don waders over my PJs, grab my

This is AFC Pepe and the author freezing at the duck blind. After fifteen-year-old Pepe made his retrieve out of the icy water, I took him to the house and wrapped him in a blanket. (Photo by Jim Culbertson)

shotgun, go out the back door, and flip the kennel gate to release two gun dogs. In four minutes I'd be heading for the duck blind.

Every dawn.

Never change.

Day after day after day – during legal season – for seven years.

"Lucky," you say.

"Mighty," I answer.

All I had to do to get all this was give up my position in the arena of man – forfeit my head start in the human race. It just became more important for me to know a duck than to make a buck. To learn to decipher the mysteries of nature, instead of the quirks of the stock market. To develop the skills required to break the chain of survival that took species millions of years to develop, rather than learn how to win friends and influence people. To be able to enter nature on its own terms and compete and win. Not to excel in the eyes of man, but in my own way of thinking and in nature's way of testing.

To develop, for the first time in my life – in something as fundamental as life and death – *a reason to have faith in myself.* To finally be good at something – alone. Maybe this is the reason the poor so love to hunt. They who own nothing and control nothing suddenly have that which escapes all but a few – that ability to be in control of nature.

Year after year the hunt took a deeper meaning for me, but shooting became less and less a priority. It finally got to the point where I'd leave the house and en route to the blind figure out the day's rotation. If the ducks did not come in mallard, pintail, greenwing teal, widgeon (in that order), I could not shoot. And if those species *did arrive* in succession, I still couldn't shoot unless there was a drake. No hens were ever brought to hand.

Ducks don't generally fly on a rainy day. Nor do you see them about in the fog. And decoys frozen all askew in the ice don't usually draw ducks. But dawn after dawn I would go to the blind with two dogs; I knew there'd be no shoot, but there would be a hunt.

Always the hunt: that's what drew me. And still does. To hear my breathing as I walked, a form of a tune hushed out in vapor, the swish of my rubber boots in wet grass, the clanking of dog whistles and duck calls as they swung on their separate lanyards, the rustle of rubberized canvas in my poncho. The smell of green meadow and cow dung and rotting wood in the orchard. The rivulets of water streaming down my cheeks. The running of my nose. The chance sighting of a coon slinking in the grass, the heat of the stool rising in the mist, the stench of it drowning my nostrils.

Then, I would arrive at the duck blind to pull the stadium seats from between the hay bales and sit on frozen plastic. Place my feet on

FC and AFC Keg of Black Powder, the greatest hunting retriever I ever met. Powder belonged to Jim Culbertson, and the two of them formed a powerful harvesting machine. This painting was done by artist and Mearns quail hunter Jim Pettijohn. (Photo by Harry Schraeder)

wood flats used by forklifts in warehouses. Open the thermos and fill the metal cup, knowing to pour just a little over the rim so I could put it to my lips. But never knowing why that worked.

Peering now to see if the decoys rode well. None sinking. None pulled down by the neck, tangled by anchor cord. Fouled decoys will flare flights. Ducks know. They spot a phony rig in a second.

The sun comes up smoked scarlet, casting vague shadows across the pond. Now a crow flies past, scolding my intrusion. Two songbirds twitter in the bare branches. They do not see me and frolic as children.

No duck will come this morning. But that's the point. No need for a duck to come for me to hunt. To smell, to feel, to see, to suppose, to figure, and to imagine – these are the components of hunting. Not a mad dash, a stumbling, a cry, a barrage of bullets, or a blood-letting. That's not hunting, that's slaughtering. Game is sacred to me. It deserves a chance to survive. But if it must die, let it be the last note in a symphony, the last step in a ballet, the last stroke in a painting. Let the hunter deserve it. And honor it. And approach it with skill and devotion. The bird has earned this.

Now I discern the pattern in the ice, watch an elm leaf spiral, hear a pheasant launch across the pond, see the red-tailed hawk ride a thermal – peering down for his breakfast. An odd black bug climbs the Sudan grass matting I've woven. The wind rises and the frozen branches crack like peanut brittle. This is to hunt; not to find game, but to find one's self. To learn who you are and what world you live in. To be far from the maddening crowd so you can, at last, listen, see, hear, feel, and, inevitably, pray.

To say it simply, man must learn his game and his gun and his dog and his land and his water so well that he enters it silent and natural as a snake. He comes with no commotion, no fanfare, no display.

He must also know his quarry. Know it so well that he can enter nature where the bird is supreme and dupe it to come to his call, be tricked by his decoys, be guided to his gun. And then, to shoot or not to shoot. For the hunt is the tricking, see. You know you've won if the bird comes into range. That is the test. Shooting can be proven with a tin can. But only a hunter can outwit game to come within range. That's hunting.

Understand?

I'll give one further explanation.

But one moment. While I've got you here, let me continue with our nonshooting duck hunter above. He does not just hunt ducks during duck season. He hunts them all year. How?

Well, first of all, he must make his own decoys. And then learn to paint them. And be engineer enough to make them float like a bird.

Professional retriever trainer Jim Charlton of Portland, Oregon, with the leapingest, birdiest golden I ever met. Traditionally known as an upland game–retrieving specialist, this golden is a water wizard.

Then he plants the tall grass, which he'll scythe in the fall to weave his wrap-around duck blind. Plus, there is always the training of the duck dogs. And the building of the duck boat. And the duck call, too.

And the practice with the gun. If you're going to shoot, hit what you shoot at and hit it hard and honest and sure. A cripple is a testimonial to a man's deficiency: an automatic cancellation of nature's ticket to play the game.

So there's never an end to duck season. Why, there's the field trial to win with Pup. The training him and drilling him and conditioning him every day. The International Decoy Championship at Davenport, Iowa, to enter. The duck boat races at the Michigan Duck Hunter's Tournament, the layout boat shoot, the duck plucking, the duck calling, the marsh race in chest waders where anything goes. To enter (and lose) the World Duck Calling Contest held each winter at Stuttgart, Arkansas.

You see?

There are summer hours spent in the marsh, watching the hatch, the molt, the early flights. Learning to identify waterfowl by their silhouettes so you know them up close. Or by their flight characteristics so you can identify them a half-mile distant.

Loading your own shells. Operating your own trap. All these things are woven into the fabric of year-round duck hunting.

Coming by a small piece of property and planting your own Wapato duck potato, Japanese millet, Sudan, milo, lespedeza, corn. Or doing good things for a farmer in exchange for his planting these things. Or petitioning your state legislature to get it done on public land.

And supporting your Ducks Unlimited, Quail Unlimited, Pheasants Forever – all the conservation efforts that have helped increase game, probably tenfold, during this century.

And finally, learning how to dress, cook, and serve wild game. Not wasting a morsel. If you harvested that bird, you must thank God for its life, and like the American Indian dedicate that life to the sustenance of your own.

But before I was interrupted, I was going to offer you a further illustration.

Super Scooper of Vondalia, a long-legged, full-bored-nosed, slim-built Lab who once won a seventy-five-dog derby at Saint Louis, was leading me down a dike at Cheyenne Bottoms one morning: a great flat skillet of a place in central Kansas where the Arkansas River tips over the spillways and keeps the place flooded. It is a waterfowl mecca.

Scoop and I were walking in the dark, heading for our blind, when one after another the dog fetched up and delivered to hand some crippled bird a slaughterer (not a bird hunter, mind you) had shot and crippled the day before and left to die. I would take the bird, and when Scoop wasn't looking drop it along the dike. If a game warden caught me with a shot bird in possession before legal shooting time, I would have been arrested.

I was perturbed at the wealth of ducks Scoop presented me, feeling sorry for the cripples and wanting to pinch the head off the guy who shot and left them, when suddenly, out of the dark, I nearly bumped into an old man who was standing on the dike. He seemed like layered clay, dressed in home-vulcanized waders, a canvas coat out at the elbows, and a grimed cap. He carried a Model 12 shotgun with the barrel worn pewter gray.

"Oh, I'm sorry," I managed to say.

The man shook his head – nodding he understood.

I paused a second, than offered, "Gotta be going . . . hope you get your limit."

The old man was silent for a moment, then said in a wispy voice, "My need is more to see them than to shoot."

And that's one of the first times I sensed what it meant to be a hunter.

Super Scooper of Vondalia, the author's derby champion, with a Canada goose taken from a farm pond. Scoop never made it on the big open field-trial circuit because he refused to sit anywhere his testicles would get wet.

Okay, we're ready to start this book. We've talked about ducks here in the introduction, but all gamebirds will get equal attention. We'll describe the bird you seek and explain his characteristics, his routines, and his habits. Then we'll show you how to handle your gun dog either to find the bird and present him to the gun or fetch him to hand after the shot.

If it has to do with bird, dog, gun, we'll be doing it. As we tell Pup in the morning, "Hie on." That means let's get going.

1

The Great American Bird Hunting Expedition

THERE IS AN engine to the hunt. It's built of guns, dogs, boots, boats, shells, bells, and all the other stuff that makes up this greatest American outing.

To build a hunting engine (and become its engineer), you must buy a gun, dog, boots, boat, shells, bells, and then – in order – practice with the gun, train the dog, break in the boots, paddle the boat, recognize the bell (around the neck of your dog), and get the whole machine running.

That's when we go hunting. With the lights flashing, the boiler stoked, the drive wheels turning – NOW WE'RE GETTING SOME-WHERE.

But first, we must assemble and learn how to use all this hardware. We must take the time to build the engine. No other way will it work. Then, and only then, can the rest of the book be what we want – JUST FOR THE BIRDS!

Dogs

The world of gun dogs is made up of bird dogs, retrievers, flushers, and mutts. Bird dogs point birds, retrievers fetch them, flushers knock birds out of their hide, and mutts – often with amazing, hybrid vigor – do it all. We don't talk of blue bloods here: we talk of gun dogs.

In all my gun-dog life, the finest dog who ever took me hunting was a three-quarter English pointer, one-quarter German shorthaired pointer named George. He had one ear only; as a pup his daddy had bit the other one off. This was a road-hunting dog, working out of the back of a pickup, breaking at the sound of the safety. He hunted for a man named Gyp who shot a Western Auto shotgun with a sawed-off barrel. The front sight consisted of a penny-pencil red eraser held on top the barrel with electrical tape. Now, that's not fancy, and it sure ain't classic, but this dog and this man put meat on the table. And friends, that's what this book is about. Okay?

Bird Dogs

There are two truly great bird dogs: the pointers and the setters, the slicks and the shags.

They both trace back to Spain by way of England, and who knows where else. Remember, England gave us most all of our field sports as well as the hardware, animals, ethics, and rules to play by.

English pointers are prototypically tall, slender, long-nosed dogs with high bone balconies, soft folding ears, stout muzzles, dark, rich

This is one-eared George, the bobwhite journeyman. I'll bet George found and brought more quail to hand than any dog who ever lived.

Four-time Champion Bozeann's Mosely is probably the greatest English setter to scorch the field-trial scene since Gladstone. Furthermore, he has sired more field-trial winners than any other setter in history. He is trialed, hunted, and scrimmaged in football by his owners, Loyd and Ruth Bozeman of Nettleton, Mississippi. (Photo by Ruth Bozeman)

eyes, prominent rib cages, great heart girth, and dynamic pelvic drive muscles. They are short-haired.

English setters are everything above, with curls.

Irish setters are everything above, with a luxurious red coat.

Red setters are an authorized Field Dog Stud Book outcross of an Irish and an English setter. They are becoming very popular in America.

Now, when I say one thing in this book, I also say another. Yes, some pointers have hair too long, and some setters look naked. I have a Currier and Ives print of an English setter that's wooly as a bear and just about as bulky. That's just the way it is when you enter God's kingdom and build a hunting engine. Like I say, retrievers retrieve. It may well be that the English setter you have is the best retriever in all the world—if you keep the water warm. Right? Okay?

Now the value of gun dogs is they lead you afield and hunt for birds, which they detect with a miracle nose. They then stand solid while you get in position to take your shots when the bird finally flushes.

But not all pointers started out that way. Some came to us hunting fur, not feather. These are primarily German dogs. And there are a slew of them: German shorthaired pointer, German roughhaired pointer, German wirehaired pointer, German longhaired pointer, pudelpointer, and wirehaired pointing griffon, to name a few. I could go on and on, but there are also dogs from other countries like vizslas, weimeraners, and Brittanies. The purist could say that the Brittany isn't a pointer at all, but a flusher. Yet, a Brittany beat all the slicks and shags that appeared one year in the grueling three-hour International Gun Dog Endurance Championship. So I repeat. Pay attention to what I say, but know I can mean something else, too. Nevertheless, bird dogs point birds. We can be 90 percent sure.

Now for the Flushers

Flushers take hunters to field and run ahead—vigorously, animatedly, joyously, and with a near-compulsive drive—to come upon a hidden bird and literally throw themselves onto it. The bird squawks, staggers, leaps, and flaps, and sometimes the flushing dog has the feathered tail in his mouth as the bird flies away. Now all this time the hunter, who must have the reaction time of an Indy-car driver, is

A popular hunting dog of today is the German short-haired pointer. This is the real McCoy, photographed in Germany while duck hunting with his professional trainer.

whipping up his gun, swinging, aiming, firing, and then smiling as his dog casts to fetch what he shot. Yes, flushers make excellent fetchers.

You will know a flushing dog when you see an English springer spaniel, Welsh springer spaniel, American or English cocker spaniel, clumber spaniel, Sussex spaniel, or field spaniel.

In other words, flushers are spaniels. These can be medium-size, or even small, vest-pocket dogs. Whatever space they take up, it's occupied mostly by heart, a little hind end, some legs, a fluff of hair, two great flowing ears, mellow eyes, a coat you can't stop stroking, and a tail that won't stop wagging.

Lucky the man with a flusher. He's given birds afield and a warm night abed.

Retrievers

Retrievers are the drive wheels of the engine. They are bulky, big-shouldered, broad-headed, strong-built, close-coupled, and heavy-tailed (which honestly serves as a rudder). They have web feet for swimming, a waterproof coat, and a disposition to make Job look hyper. Retrievers are mellow.

There's nothing like a Lab, or a Chesie, or a flat-coated retriever, or a curly-coated retriever, or a golden retriever, or an American water or Irish water spaniel (spaniel? there we go again, another contradiction) to sleep before your fireplace or break ice in getting you a duck. Yes, water is their specialty.

Emerging as the top Chesapeake Bay retriever trainer in America today is Jeff Devazier of Stuttgart, Arkansas. A Chesie will fetch your duck from wave-crested ice caps and then guard it for you. No one ever took anything away from a Chesie.

With a pair of Labs up front, the late John Olin (of Winchester fame), retired retriever trainer Cotton Pershall, and driver follow two mules to bobwhite at the Nilo Plantation. John had an aluminum wagon tongue made for the mules so it wouldn't be so heavy.

They are the swellest of fellows, and if all men had retrievers' hearts, there'd never be a discouraging word.

But that's not all. Today the emphasis is on the hunting retriever. This dog also leads you afield, detects the hidden quarry, and delay-points (or leaps) to flush (depending on how he was trained) while you position yourself to shoot the bird. Then, the retriever fetches, marks down deadfall, goes for whatever was shot, and continues with the hunt.

In the many years I've trained dogs I can honestly say most of them can do it all: seek, find, hold, fetch, and continue. After all, that's how they made their living a long time before they ever threw in with man.

And speaking of that, the American Indians told their white-eyed captors, "God made the earth, the sky and water, moon and sun. He made man and bird and beast. But He didn't make the dog. He already had one."

You're the richest of all men if you've got one, too.

Lock, Stock, and Barrel

Hunters harvest birds with shotguns. Which means the gun does not shoot a single projectile, but a multitude. There are several shotguns to choose from: the pump, semiautomatic, bolt-action, and hinged (over-and-under, side-by-side, or single barrel). Incidentally, if the semiautomatic shotgun is ever outlawed by a simplistic-thinking public and a knee-jerk government, we will have to go to a hinged gun, either over-and-under or side-by-side. To look at the bright side (if there is any), we'll be giving up only one shot per encounter since most states have long required hunters to plug a semiautomatic's magazine so it can hold only three shells at a time.

Shells

Shot pellets (lead, copper-coated lead, or steel) are encased in a shot shell stored in the shotgun's magazine (pump, semiautomatic, or bolt-action) or in the chamber (hinged gun). Shot pellets are generally sized from BB to No. 9 (the latter being the smallest). A shell containing No. 9 shot in a 1¼-ounce load will contain 731 pellets; a No. 6 shot load will contain 281 shot pellets; and No 4. shot load will produce 169 shot pellets.

The pattern of shot is determined by many factors, but most importantly by the choke of the gun barrel. Choke refers to the degree of constriction in the bore at the muzzle, which affects the range of the gun. There are essentially six popular chokes: cylinder, for a range of 15 yards; skeet, for 20; improved-cylinder, for 25; modified, for 35; improved-modified, for 40; and full for 50.

Of course, there are other factors at work. Barrel gauge, for example. We generally shoot 12-gauge guns, which have an inside bore diameter of .730 inch; 20-gauge guns have a bore diameter of .615; 28-gauge has a bore diameter of .550 inch; and 67-gauge (or .410) has a bore diameter of .410 inch.

We use No 4. shot for long-range and pass shooting. For row-crop shooting, where long shots at distant birds such as pheasants are common, try No. 5. For the customary covey rise before dogs, use No. 6, except for the far-reaching bird where one No. 4 may be placed to come up last in the chamber.

Always wear shooting glasses and earplugs afield. What could be more precious than your sight and hearing?

Ducks require a sequence of No. 6s and No. 4s—getting the late flyers as they are going away requires heavier shot.

On ruffed grouse, Hungarian partridge, and exotic quail, 7½s and 8s are popular loads. Same goes for doves. Woodcock will see the shot in sizes 7½, 8, and 9. Geese call for No. 4s, or bigger. There is a No. 2 for geese, and a BB, if all else falls short. But now you're sky-busting.

And finally there's length of barrel; that, too, determines range and general effectiveness. Most barrels are found in 26- through 32-inch lengths. The longer the barrel, the tighter the shot string; which means the longer the effective load holds together. The shorter the barrel, the more a pattern develops nearer the end of the muzzle. That gives you maximum shot at a close target.

To give you a better idea of what's happening with all this firepower, consider that when you shoot a modified choke (that's a popular one), you'll find that No. 6s go 35 yards, No. 4s go 40 yards, and No. 9s go 25 yards. Now those ranges are for lead shot. It's important for you to understand that steel shot is required for *all* waterfowl in the United States. Some states require its use on upland game as well. Always check the regulations. In steel-shot zones, you cannot have *any* lead shot in possession—either in the gun or on your person. Make sure you check all pockets in jackets and pants for errant lead shells.

New to the market at the time of this writing are the nontoxic

If you have the time, make your own duck calls. At least practice with whatever calls you have so you can experience the thrill of calling ducks to your set.

Bismuth shot pellets marketed by the Bismuth Cartridge Co. of Dallas, Texas. (In mid-1993, this shot had not been determined legal for waterfowl by the U.S. Fish and Wildlife Service.) Bismuth pellets are about halfway between steel and lead in density; thus, they need to be about one size larger than lead – or one shot size smaller than steel. Bismuth shells are bloody expensive, and the patterning capability of these shells has not been determined. Their value lies in being a non-toxic substitute for steel shot.

Also there is a new tracer load coming out of Las Vegas, Nevada. I've been told each shell contains six white pellets that are visible the length of the shot string. This is invaluable for waterfowl hunters – they'll now know where their shot is going: whether they're shooting behind the bird, under, or over. If shooting in front, they are probably connecting. Also these tracers will prove a boon to skeet, trap, and Sporting Clay shooters.

But back to steel. In steel shot, with modified choke, a No. 6 will travel 30 yards, a No. 4 will go 42½ yards, and because we've got to go to larger pellets for greater firepower with steel, a BB will travel 50½ yards.

Now put all this together. Gauge, choke, shot size (steel or lead), and on and on. I also should mention something else; you can have either high-brass or low-brass shells . . . and different grains of powder per shell for different wallops.

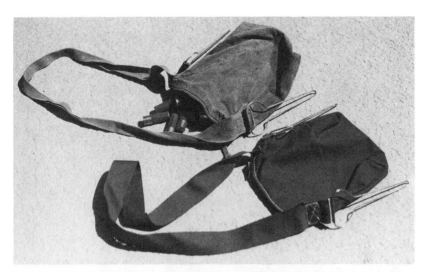

A bird hunter needs functional equipment; fancy's fine, but it don't harvest game. On top here is the author's beat-up game bag bought for $2.00 in a war surplus store. It's so good a pro dog trainer had the lower one made for himself.

That's why I said above: first you buy the gun, then you practice. You don't have anything with just the hardware.

You've got to become an operator. To learn how to pick up the gun, swing, aim, fire, and follow through – or snap, as some fellows say and do.

In this regard, the smartest thing you can do during the summer months is pattern your gun with different loads from various manufacturers. Yes, there's a mighty difference. One 12-gauge shell in your gun may fire a pattern with a distinct hole at the top right. That's the shot you're hoping connects with a goose's head. But another 12-gauge shell made by a different manufacturer may cover a whole standard 30-inch pattern with no vacant areas. Which means, hopefully, no misses.

To pattern your shotgun, take a 40 x 40-inch piece of butcher paper or newsprint and staple it to a target frame, board, or stilts. Draw a 30-inch circle in the middle of the paper. Make a mark in the center of the circle. This will be our target.

Move down range to a distance that is average for most of your shooting. For example, if most of your hunting is done on ducks, your target will be some 40 to 50 yards away. That's because this hunter's gun must deliver its best pattern at long ranges.

But should you hunt bobwhite quail, then walk away some 30 yards and test your 7½s.

You seek great density of pattern within the 30-inch circle. Other-

This is King, a field-trial whiz. I love his intensity and style, yet his face shows no giddiness; instead it shows a seasoned dog doing a calm and thorough job of holding a bird. King is in Charles Gentry's kennels in Jackson, Tennessee. (Photo by Charles Gentry)

wise, you'll be either missing targets or wounding game. If your shotgun shell is not giving you that density, you must test other manufacturers' products. Or, you must change guns.

Whatever, and however, it takes time, patience, and diligence to get ready with your shotgun. And it's mighty important: if you don't know what you're doing, you can hurt yourself, kill your dog, or wound your best friend. Just as bad, to my way of thinking, you may leave a lot of crippled game to die and be picked apart by carp or crow. Know what you're doing.

Puttin' on the Dog

The last thing we must do before starting our GREAT AMERICAN BIRD HUNTING EXPEDITION is get you and Pup ready for the field. He needs his collar, you need your kerchief—and all the other stuff that makes a hunt effective and enjoyable.

Pup

There's a ton of stuff you can buy for Pup, and for the most part you just wasted your money. All he really needs is a plain, wide, strong collar with a welded D-ring (nylon for a water dog, leather if he's after upland game). Either way, have a tag engraved with your address and phone number to tell the world this is your dog. To the collar we attach a nylon or leather leash — with a snap-swivel for the retriever or a 22-foot nylon check cord for the bird dog.

If Pup's going to be hunting in goathead, cactus, or cut-stubble country, outfit him with rubber boots. There's a special way to put these on. Slip on one boot and mark the spot where the top of the boot touches Pup's ankle. Wrap the ankle with tape 1 inch above and 1 inch below the spot. Do the same with the other ankles.

When you slide on a boot, tape it in place, applying tape to tape, which spares Pup from the fur-pulling ordeal when it's time to remove the boots. The tape should last about two weeks.

Of course, you need a first-aid kit for Pup. A good one. I've written in *Field & Stream* for two decades how (and why) to make these things up. The information's also repeated in many of my books. In addition to the kit, you'll also need some other worthwhile items.

Buy the upland game dog a pair of toenail clippers. A dog with a split nail is finished for the hunt. Don't piddle with it. Snip it completely off. That way Pup can go on hunting and still get out of his crate running the next morning.

Mrs. David Hasinger, red setter enthusiast, walks up behind her favorite male on point. The red setter is the result of an authorized outcross by the Field Dog Stud Book to mate an Irish setter with an English setter. The beget is a great bird dog with a superlative nose and long-feathered beauty. (Photo by David Hasinger)

Don't forget the distaff when it comes to straight shootin' and top-of-the-game dog handling. This little Lab took a line to the duck and brought it to hand at a Southern Arkansas Hunting Retriever Club outing.

You also need a pair of wire cutters. There is always a chance that Pup will hang up on a hog-wire, or five-strand barbed-wire fence and die from panic-stricken trauma or asphyxiation. Don't rush to him without the cutters. This dog will bite – and bite mighty. Cut him loose and keep your distance.

That's not to say you won't need the cutters for retrievers, too. I've cut more than one dog loose from an abandoned trotline.

Pheasant dogs require special care afield. Pheasants love row crops, which means rich dirt that goes to dust when dry and disturbed. Row crops are also dust and pollen holders, and when shaken, powder the dog's eyes, nose, and mouth. If there are no puddles or creeks about, carry a lot of water. Water the dog often and groom him to remove debris. One special tip: pull his bottom eye lid out and pour it full of clean water. Watch the debris puddle up next to his nose. Wipe this away with your handkerchief.

Grouse hunters and others after Huns, bobwhites, and/or the exotic quail may want their dog wearing a bell on the collar so it can always be located. You also may want to use one of the new electronic transmitting collars that tells the handler where the dog is and what he's doing. By the way, the next state-of-the-art will be the dog tracker:

I've always liked Brittanies in the field and in the house. They can do it all: scour the ground for upland game, then turn around and fetch your dove or duck. That's my gold snipe Baretta behind the Brit.

Joan Bailey of Hillsboro, Oregon, takes in the sun with a wirehaired pointing griffon. Joan is probably responsible for the popularity of this great hunting dog in America; she's been secretary of the griffon club for 30 years. The term griffon *once meant peasant festival and later anything uncivilized. In other words, these dogs came from the people, not from gentry. The first ones came from Italy, through the Alps, and into Germany.*

the same instrument used by game biologists to keep in constant contact with released wild game.

Transport Pup afield in your car or pickup. Don't ever put him in the trunk of a car. He can die. Buy an enclosed crate to store your retriever so he doesn't shake mud and water all over your car's interior. The open-screen crate is great for the upland game dog. So's the flip-flop dog waterer. Turn it one way the water's trapped, turn it another and Pup can drink.

I always buy a janitorial mat (a long runner) and put it under the crates. Unrolled, it will fling out over the tailgate of a wagon to keep Pup from tracking debris inside and scratching the hardware with his toenails.

Now don't get tricked, bamboozled, or taken. I've seen raincoats sold for retrievers so they won't get wet when they're not in the water making a retrieve. *Phew!*

How about ball caps with visors for upland dogs? Sunglasses?

Remember what I say: just because man no longer understands his place in the universe, don't let him assume all God's creatures have become equally confused and trivial. The dog just needs you, the country, and the bird. Get to it.

Dressing the Hunter

No matter what type hunting you do—peccary to polar bear—always go layered. That is, dress in one take-off garment after another: over and over.

At dawn, there'll be frost on the ground and a cold, penetrating stillness that settles between your shoulder blades. I've had this same air numb my cheeks, freeze my thighs, and water my eyes. So we dress warm.

Then, as we move about and the day warms, we start shedding. The secret is *we can never sweat.* A sweat-stroked wind chills, and chill tightens you up like a rain-swollen, paper shotgun shell. Plus it can give you pneumonia. So at the first sign of sweat . . . off comes the first outer garment. You proceed hunting, until that telltale sweat appears again, and once more you shed. You do so down to your undershirt if it gets that warm. Carry your surplus clothing in a backpack.

We each have different climes and metabolism, but generally I find the first item off is a neckerchief, then a jacket, followed by a down vest, and finally a button-up sweatshirt.

Hunting retriever clubs have great training sessions. Here the barbecue smokes up north Louisiana as the retriever handlers sample a gourmet's delight. If you want a great retriever, join a hunting retriever club.

A word about the neckerchief. Sure, some strangers think you're putting on the dog by sporting such an accessory. But they're showing their ignorance and their provincialism. That neckerchief is the best thermal garment you own. Not only does it insulate your throat, but miraculously it holds in the heat generated by your body and trapped by your shirt, sweat cardigan, down vest, and jacket. Plus, it's mighty handy to wipe your brow the rest of the day, and when soaked in water it helps groom Pup's eyes after the day's hunt.

As for pants, look for and buy some with a leather, nylon, waxed, or some other kind of tough-stuff facing that covers the front. You also can buy chaps. These garments knock away stubble and briar, and also keep you dry. Otherwise you'll end a weekend's outing with legs scaled like a turkey.

Boots now come in hundreds of configurations. Buy what you want. But heed the voice of experience: Get the featherweights for pheasants, scaled quail, and chukars. You've got miles to go before you sleep.

You want more support? Okay. Get the heavy-duty jobs with the clodhopper toes. But figure it up. Three pounds per boot and a 3-foot step, repeated how many times in 6 miles? That's more weight-lifting than I care to do. The purpose of the outing is to hunt birds, not outdo some video workout.

And finally, a word about color. Wear Blaze Orange. Its bright, glowing orange color is now seen in many garments but most generally in vests and billed caps.

Hunt twenty years and the oddsmakers at Las Vegas will wager you get sprinkled with shot – if not actually whacked. You can greatly reduce those odds by wearing Blaze Orange.

By the way, wear earplugs to avoid noise-induced hearing loss and shooting glasses to ward off eye injuries. And a lip protector to avoid cold sores. Spray yourself with repellent to stink away demons of the swamp, mountain, and desert. Wear DEET for ticks: no need tempting Lyme disease. Sunscreen is critical for those with fair skin.

I'll close with this. I know I'm simple as dirt and dense as rock. But, I admit it. So you'll not be surprised when I tell you I prefer clothes made of things given us by God. Why, the original garment was a fig leaf: that's the ultimate in camouflage.

The comfortable field clothes I wear come mainly from fur, feather, down, leather, wool, silk, and cork bark with grass or linen woven into a safari hot-weather hat. Sure, man has done the miraculous with some of his synthetics. And they're all the rage. But not for

Bill Berlat of Tucson and his stocky Chesie, Gunner, prepare breakfast on a turkey hunt in the White Mountains of northeast Arizona. No, Gunner doesn't hunt turkeys, he guards the wagon. Make plans to cook afield on your next outing: it's great fun and the eatin' is better than anywhere else.

me. The important thing with most natural fabrics is that they breathe. They not only vent the body, but they enhance silent movement as well. The American Indian in a loincloth on a pinto pony would sure played Billy Hell with a knight on horseback in tin-can armor. Heh?

And Finally

Game can never be wasted, so in this book we learn how to cook. None of that heavy, bland European kind of cooking, but quick, delicious, primarily outdoor-cooked fowl. Nothing enhances a hunt like being an expert with bird and fire.

2

The Ring-necked Pheasant

The pheasant is the only bird I know that when hunted, will, in turn, hunt you. Not to meet you, but to avoid you. To gauge your path and time your movement and assume your skill, and then use this thimble of knowledge to crow at another dawn.

MOST GAMEBIRDS WILL trust to their plumage to be one with the earth and then hesitate too long before a dog's nose. Others will drift to the call, some to the decoy, and others to bait. But not the China bird. He is born of the same blood as a fighting cock, and he does not come to hand without a scrap. He is in feather what the elephant, lion, and Cape buffalo are in hide. He knows man; he hates him and will double back on him—not to kill him as animals will—but to outwit him and leave him standing with poised gun and wilted pride.

Except for the turkey, sage grouse, sandhill crane, and some geese, the ringneck pheasant is our largest gamebird. Even that's misleading, since 22 to 23 inches of his total 36-inch length can be in tail feathers.

A cock can weigh 4 to 5 pounds, and he's mostly meat. His white breast can dry when oven-roasted (white meat cooks faster than dark meat, which means it dries faster than dark meat). So pheasants usually require some moisture in cooking.

Now the basic meat-and-potato guy (and most hunters are) wants his pheasant quartered, battered with flour and egg, blanketed in garlic, marinated in beer, and deep-fat fried. And that's excellent.

But I've learned that if you want something outstanding for company, then consider the following.

Section the pheasant. Now prepare the marinade: 1 cup tequila, 2 cups water, 6 limes (quartered and squeezed), 4 chopped garlic cloves, 4 chopped mild peppers, 1 tbls. salt, ½ tsp. pepper, ½ tsp. dry mustard, and ½ cup diced parsley or cilantro.

Let the bird sit in the marinade for 12 hours. Cook, covered, in a 350-degree oven for 45 minutes, then uncover and baste with sauce. Cook covered for 25 more minutes. Baste with sauce once more. Cook covered for 10 minutes and serve.

The sauce is made of ½ cup honey, 1 tsp. sweet basil, 3 garlic cloves (pressed), ½ tsp. salt, ¼ cup butter. If you want to go the trouble, and I do, add the pulp of 3 oranges.

The Pheasant's Plymouth Rock

Pheasants are not found everywhere in the United States. They are a farm-belt bird, though their first successful import was to Corvallis, Oregon. The American Consul General in Shanghai—Judge Owen Denny—shipped twenty-one or thirty (I've heard both figures) ringnecks to his brother's farm. I once lived in Oregon and remember the

Professional world champion wildlife carver (plus painter and sculptor) William J. Koelpin of Wauwatosa, Wisconsin, renders a trio of pheasants almost better than nature can do it. (Photo by Mark Deprez)

Willamette Valley as a lush, wet place known for truck farming. The birds survived.

Seven years later, the Rutherford-Stuyvesant estate in Alamuchy, New Jersey, imported a Scottish gamekeeper and his family, who also brought pheasants with them. The birds caught on here as well – New Jersey is another garden environment.

Some game biologists tell us there has to be a particular amount of lime in the soil to sustain pheasants. The laying hen requires more calcium than birds native to this country. At any rate, you'll find pheasants in a bowed triangle that runs from Maine south of the Great Lakes, north into Canada, and all the way to Oregon. The southern leg cuts through mid-America and dips into New Mexico. The base of the triangle runs from northern California into Canada, though there is a spot in the southeast tip of California that can support pheasants. With but odd exceptions, there's not a pheasant in those states that once made up the Confederacy. The pheasant range also roughly follows that country scoured by the ice-age glaciers. In this scattering, the greater number of birds are brought to hand in Iowa. Which indicates pheasants may survive in garden country, but their population explodes on corn.

Mirror, Mirror on the Wall

In this book we'll use only field identifications of gamebirds. By that I mean a bird in hand may look like a bird in escape flight (which is the way we'll be seeing them here and in the field), but not always. The most distinguishing thing about a cock pheasant in hand could well be the blood-red patch about his eyes and the iridescent plumage of his head. But that's not what you see when this bird flushes. Instead, you see three things. First, a large dirt-colored bird, big as a raven; second, a twitter of tail feathers, which look to be writhing snakes; and third, the white ring about the pheasant's neck.

That white ring is especially visible to the road hunter who sees the ring disappear in the weed-clogged ditch just as the pheasant ducks his head. Being late has cost many a bird his life.

Of course, there's that breathtaking chance sighting of thirty-six cocks standing on bright green winter wheat just as a glaring sun is setting. Then those vivid red eye patches glow like maraschino cherries, and the puffed-up breasts of these gallants is hammered copper. I hope you see it some day; it's only happened to me a dozen times in forty-five years of hunting.

There is no confusing cocks with hens. The latter is a drab bird the color of dirt. And though the cock can call out raucous and loud as a circus barker, the female is relatively mute. She is stub-tailed and puffy in appearance. And, interesting to note, she seldom watches a fight between suitors for her favor, but she always leaves with the winner. And that cock usually has the longest tail and the brightest red cheek patch.

The male usually assembles a harem of six hens, each of whom tends eleven or twelve eggs. Consequently, the sport hunter could harvest six cocks to every hen. But beware, the cock pheasant is a chauvinistic bird who maintains no fidelity to his harem; he'll prod them to flight before he'll leave cover. So remember: nine times out of ten the first birds up are hens. DON'T SHOOT!

Prince and Pauper

The pheasant is a very strange bird. He's beautiful enough to denote

Startled by an exploding cock pheasant, this hunter readies himself while the Brittany mirrors his excitement.

An overloaded Brittany totes a cock pheasant to hand. These little dogs can do it all—plus my Brits have always shared my bed.

elegance. I've seen him mounted and strutting down the table as a centerpiece in a French estate when dining with my betters after hunting pheasant outside Orleans along the Loire River. But this same bird is akin to a carnival fighter. If human, he'd have hair on his shoulders, a broken nose, and a tattoo on his chest that said something like: "Make my day."

He has fallen to my M-1 as a Marine in Korea to be boiled in a helmet with K-rations. And, in Wales, he has been driven to me as I held a borrowed Purdey, as delicate and lovely as a thoroughbred's front leg. There he was served in a fifteenth-century mansion while a string quartet played in an outer chamber.

Behind the Big Wall

When raised in captivity, pheasant beaks must be snipped or shrouded so the birds won't kill each other. Their spurs must also be removed. Remember this when sending a pup for a retrieve. Older dogs know how to handle this scrapping bird when it's merely crippled, but a pup can be ruined as a retriever for life with just one pugnacious encounter.

And though cock pheasants have a death wish for each other during mating season or while penned up—nevertheless, the pheasant is a communal bird. Often you'll find flocks of thirty or more holed up in the same thicket.

How to Hunt

There are essentially two ways to hunt this bird. A group of hunters can walk abreast through a row crop, driving the birds before them, to be encountered by blockers at the end of the field who are also armed. The birds are simply bottled up and when they loft, they're shot. Pheasants have a deep reluctance to leave cover, so anytime you drive the bird before you it is known he'll probably take flight at any edge.

Pheasants are also hunted by one or two men (or women: this will be understood henceforth and not stated) with a dog or dogs who literally hunt the bird the way they'd go for bobwhites. Yet, pheasants are not inclined to sit to point. Consequently, the best dog tactic is to have an English springer spaniel who chases the bird down, leaps, and lofts him to the gun. Another equally good method is to put down a hunting retriever on whistle and hand signals. Cast the retriever out and around the bird's assumed location and work the dog back into the gun – once again trapping the bird. (You're actually driving the bird to you as you give the retriever the come-in whistle.)

This does not mean the bird can't be pinned down and kicked to flight. This happens often in great mounds of tumbleweeds where the birds hole up, thinking they're safe, only to have you barge in – or your dog cast in – and the birds explode.

Pheasants fly only as a last consequence: a trait that has earned them the epithet of "chicken bird" by nonadmirers. Like falconers, who despise pheasants because they'll run and duck under a barbed-wire fence that can badly mangle a falcon who dives for them. The falconers say the bird should stand and fight like a prairie chicken, who attempts to outmaneuver the falcon in open combat.

Well anyway, pheasants are reluctant to fly, and you'll see them run before you, like dust-colored ghosts with packs on their backs. The back just naturally humps up. And they'll run so long as you move. But there's a trick, especially in rattling row crops. Just stop, don't make a sound. Stand there for five minutes. Sometimes the suspense gets too much for the bird, and he'll either blunder into view or launch, giving you a shot.

Yet, there is another hole card up the China bird's sleeve. That's his doubling back. You think you've got him bottled up, you think he's being herded, and then up he comes – 20 yards behind you or far out to side. To deal with this, have your phalanx of hunters walk in a sag, the point men being to front on either side. Then the bird must go back between you.

But you can fool him by dropping back yourself. Keep checking

Gun dog trainer, guide, and preserve operator Mike Gould of Carbondale, Colorado, swings to drop a pheasant that jumped from under an Elhew pointer's slam-down point.

your back trail, look to see movement. Or, every so often, turn about and go backwards, quartering as you do. Or, call your retriever in and cast him behind the hunting party. You may find the fugitive.

The Hunting Lab

This casting of the retriever reminds me of the excesses of my youth. Jim Culbertson of Wichita, Kansas, a fellow amateur retriever trainer at that time—it was the early 1960s—lived as I did to beat the pros. He would put his string with mine, and we could have more than ten trained Labs in the China bird patch. We could vacuum the thing sterile, launching the birds as before a prairie fire. For each dog was but an extension of our arm. They were trained that well, to have that response to the whistle and hand signals, to be that honest. We could literally reach out 40 yards and touch the bird—just as if the dog were a finger. And we could control ten fingers—and lift ten birds. Though a more reasonable number of Labs before us was four. But this madness of our youth soon left. We gradually learned that to hunt is not to shoot . . . for to shoot, if you think about it, is the end of the hunt.

The best way to train a retriever for pheasants is in an orchard, especially a pecan orchard. There you can move the dog among the evenly spaced trees like a queen on a chessboard. Once you get the dog positioned right, then call him to you. A novice dog will come back in a straight line, but an all-age dog will quarter to herd the birds to you.

And don't think some dogs can't outrun a flying pheasant. This bird is a short-flight performer. He's not built for anything else. Up he goes, levels out, soars, gives maybe one beat or two in flight, and glides to earth where he hits and runs. But a dog in pursuit will be on him soon after he lands and the bird will be obliged to fly again. Well, a pheasant just doesn't have that many touch-and-gos in him. He'll sputter, flop, and be brought to hand.

The Pheasant's House and Home

Targets of opportunity for the pheasant hunter—apart from row crops—are mounds of tumbleweeds, hedgerows, waterways (those ditches left to ground cover where fields are drained), creek banks, weeds around abandoned farm buildings, ditches along the road, and lake shores. Yet the most classic shot I ever made on a cock pheasant was from the first tee box at the Mulvane, Kansas, municipal golf course. Champion Keg of Black Powder, Jim Culbertson's immortal field-trial Lab (and hunting nut), had run off to the right in the rough and launched the bird to fly straight across the fairway. It was a hole in one.

Pheasant Dog Specialists

There's hardly a breed of gun dog I haven't taken to the pheasant field. They're all good. But a dog that can track is an asset. We're after a running quarry. If the day's not too dry and the dust not too heavy, the dog will foot-trail and eventually launch the bird. But 80 yards out does you little good when the firing range is half that distance. So the dog must be tractable to the whistle. He must leave off his forward drive when you ask him to – even if he's on the trail of hot scent.

It's been said you'll ruin a bird dog by putting him on pheasants. The bird won't hold for point, and the dog must forsake his training to relocate. Maybe. But seasoned dogs soon learn the game. Some even become so aggressive they slam down point hard enough to intimidate the bird so it'll sit there and not even think of moving.

Springer spaniel expert Bob Bullard, DVM, of Cornelius, Oregon, hups two of his many springers on the lawn after a training session. The springer is the ultimate pheasant dog.

Remember, throughout this book, throughout these hunts, every dog needs a day off, a day to play. I've had English pointers go amuck in the pheasant field to prove staunch on quail the next day. Gun dogs enjoy a new adventure as much as you do, and they're not without common sense. After all, they were making their living this way long before man ever put a collar on them. I've never had a dog that couldn't figure out the tactics of this China bird and produce feather.

Finally, there comes the day it snows, and that's when you and Pup should head for the pheasant fields. The birds leave visible tracks to start with, and you can trail them. Plus, they're not so willing to fly.

If they get wet under the wings, they can easily freeze and die. It's the pheasant's nature to turn his back to a storm wind: to driven rain or snow. The wind lifts his feathers, so the moisture gets in between the plumage and the body. And the heat of the bird melts the snow. Eventually that moisture freezes. (For this reason, don't ever forgo hunting the birds in a cold rain. Pheasants hate water; they won't want to move – even in stubble – because they'll get wet.) Consequently, the pheasant will dig under the snow, thinking he's safe. That's when your dog can have fun. Sniffing out the bird's blow hole, and diving in to either come up with bird in mouth or see the world explode as the pheasant comes squawking out.

A Bird in Hand

One of the joys of hunting is that you never know what's going to happen. We were hunting western Kansas when one of those blizzards hit, and there was this pheasant hunkered down in a bare ditch that had turned to an ice sculpture.

One of the guys jumped out of the station wagon and placed the bird in the back. Later, the bird warmed and began to move, so we opened the rear door, took him to hand, and launched him to flight.

What's that?

No, cynic, we didn't shoot.

Hunters always give more back to game than they take. If it weren't for hunters' humanity, concern, and care, their philanthropy and license and equipment fees, there'd be scant wildlife in America. Plus, hunters form together to go that extra mile for wildlife: consider conservation organizations such as Pheasants Forever, Ducks Unlimited, Quail Unlimited, and The Ruffed Grouse Society, to name a few.

When better ways are found to help wildlife, it will be the hunters who see that the programs are implemented and funded. Bird, deer, or rabbit – their first protectors are the men who hunt them.

Stowing the Bird

There's something about a pheasant that tantalizes a dog. Once the bird is in your hand, the dog will generally insist on leaping for it. So wear a vest or coat with a game pouch where you can store the bird out of sight. That's especially important if you're hunting a young pup that wants to linger and not cast out for a new hunt.

Make sure the bird is dead before stowing it. I've been spurred good by a stunned bird I put in the game pouch that later came to life, rearing and kicking.

Hunt the Edge

And there is this immutable truth for all birds. They live on the edge. *That is, 90 percent of all birds will be found in 10 percent of nature.* That 10 percent is where there is a break in flora: a hedgerow, a plum thicket in a pasture, where the soybean field touches the pine forest. Wherever habitat changes, that's where birds frequent. Don't hunt

Here they are, everybody's triumvirant: Brittany, English setter, and English pointer. Any one of these guys can do it all on upland game. Have you ever seen a prettier tail on a setter?

wide, monotonous spaces. Only a rare bird will be found there. Always hunt the edge.

Preserve Shooting

Oh, another thing. As land becomes scarce due to development, industry, or posting, hunters of the future will more and more frequent game preserves. There they will be confronted with pen-raised birds. Pheasants do well at these places, but smart operators give the client a better hunt by raising pheasant chicks in flight pens that feature the same cover they'll see when planted in the field.

That way the bird thinks he knows where he is, hides there as he has for weeks in the flight pen, and is less apt to leave the preserve. He feels comfortable in familiar habitat. All of which means to the paying customer the bird will be there to shoot once launched and not be off and away, wandering down some county road.

As years go by, you'll learn what questions to ask preserve operators to assure yourself the most realistic hunt. All of this is relatively new for us. But one of the questions will always be: "Is the bird's flight pen planted in the same cover as the field where he'll be released?"

The Pheasant Gun

Use the scattergun of your preference: we all come to the field with different backgrounds and skills. I was a Marine Corps rifleman, so I was programmed for long, concentrated shooting. That meant I naturally took to duck and pheasant hunting, where you have the far-away disappearing or crossing bird. When it came to something that flew fast and erratic, and I had to snap shoot—to react on impulse—I fumbled and faltered on such targets as woodcock, bobwhites, and ruffed grouse. That lasted until I got an ultralight, 20-gauge, automatic Franchi. I could bring that jewel up and swing it faster than a feather duster. And that's what it was: a feather duster. But we'll save that story for the king of upland birds: the bobwhite quail.

I usually hunt pheasants with a 12-gauge, field-grade, Remington 1100 auto with a 28-inch barrel and a ventilated rib, I use a full choke and 2³/₄-inch shells. I never had a more durable and accurate gun. It self-pointed and blew a dense pattern. The 1969 *Guns Illustrated* wrote, "The most dependable automatic in the world—up to 55 percent less recoil—up to seven times longer life."

And let me say this here and be done with it. You should never buy a gun from me. My guns must be the best there is to take the abuse I give them. I don't pamper myself, so I don't pamper my tools. My guns are never cleaned; they get rusty from saltwater, the stocks are scarred, the barrels are dented from falling on rocks, the chambers are scarred from my trying to pry out wet paper shells that have swollen tight. Yes, paper shells. There's no telling what you'll find in the pockets of those old hunting clothes.

The Browning Superposed shotgun, 12-gauge, 28-inch barrels, modified and improved cylinders, with ventilated rib, has always been my field-trial gun of choice. Safety is foremost around all those dogs and people, so being able to break a gun in two and look in its innards is a necessity. At the retriever trials, we shot pheasants and mallards and I was standing there all day. I wasn't lugging the thing in that tortuous mound-and-ditch terrain of a row crop. No matter how you rationalize a two-tube gun away, you're still toting an extra barrel that weighs slightly more (4 ounces more than an 1100). Shoot it all day, and an ounce is weight.

As for the pump, better be born shooting it. Otherwise, you'll have some of the weirdest experiences ever known to ballistics. My oldest shooting buddy was born with a Winchester Model 12 in his hand. He performs magic tricks with the thing. It's all what you're used to. For some, it's like a casting reel; if you can't use one and must rely on a spinning rig, then why go fishing? In other words, every class of gun has its purists, even the single shot.

Sure, it would be fancy to appear afield toting an Italian import, say a 20-gauge over-and-under with gold inlay. But I row boats with guns, use their stocks to press down barbed-wire fences, separate bramble with the barrel. For me to own that Roman heirloom would see it mint in the gun case forevermore.

As for firepower on pheasant, I load so that two low-brass 6s fire first, followed by one high-brass 4. If I miss with the maximum pellet pattern on my first two shots, I can try for the going away or crossing shot with the high-brass 4. I keep the shells separate by carrying them in opposite pockets of my jacket.

Whatever gun you carry, outfit it with a leather sling. No need balancing all that weight over a multimile walk. With practice, you can unshoulder the gun and come to firing stance in seconds. I don't speak here of the sling that requires you to install screws in the stock. No, I use the two-loop slip-on leather strap that goes over both barrel and stock without leaving a blemish.

Gun Dogs

My favorite gun dog for pheasants is the hunting Lab. I don't mean the

Here's the original Irish setter with the late John Nash on the Ballyfin moor in central Ireland. John was the sixth-generation Nash to raise these dogs. They are foxlike in agility, and some have a white blaze on the chest.

old classic field-trial Lab: the one labeled a nonslip retriever. That is, he never left your side until you slipped the collar. No. The new hunting Lab casts out in quest of game, roots it up, and launches it to flight. (Sure, I've had them bring live game to me they caught on the flush). Then after you've fired, the Lab is without peer in rooting out deadfall and delivering it to hand.

I've referred to English pointers above as doing a good job, but I'm talking about the new "self-training" English pointer as developed by Bob Wehle of Midway, Alabama, and Henderson, New York. For example, Elhew Marksman won the National Amateur Pheasant Championship, Elhew Jungle won the National Open Pheasant Shooting Dog Championship, Elhew Zeus won the National Amateur Pheasant Championship, and Elhew Huckleberry won the National Open Pheasant Shooting Dog Championship. If one dog wins one champion-

This is one of George Hickox's springers out of Nova Scotia. George is a state-of-the-art trainer of springers and Llewellyn setters, and he guides for ruffed grouse and pheasants. You need no shooter on pheasants; these springers will do it all. (Photo by George Hickox)

I was hunting ducks with this pudelpointer in Germany where the breed originated. A magnificent versatile hunting dog, the pudelpointer is preferred by me both for field and hearth.

ship that tells us little, but a string of dogs with a string of wins tells us everything.

These dogs are biddable and bred to please where the sound of your voice, your stance, and your facial expression are today's training instruments.

There's also another type of pointer that is relatively new. They are the versatile gun dogs: the European imports. This list includes the Brittany, the German shorthaired pointer, the German longhaired pointer, the German wirehaired pointer, the wirehaired pointing griffon, the pudelpointer, and others.

These dogs are ideal for pheasants for many reasons. Foremost, they have the coat for it. That dense, coarse hair turns briar and stubble, barbed wire, and thorns. They also are close-working, biddable dogs. They innately know to hunt for the gun, and they don't balk or hold grudges. They want to please; they need only to be trained and then asked to show their stuff.

Finally, they are manageable enough so they can learn to give themselves over to whistle and hand signals. They'll do your bidding no matter how far to side or front, and they will come in without brooding.

As for sheer joy, there's nothing that can equal an English springer spaniel or an English cocker. I'm talking vest-pocket power here. These guys (or gals: I prefer females in the field) have more heart than common sense. They'll literally hunt themselves to death. Plus, they are both a flusher and a retriever. They will do the entire job.

Good breeding will give you a dense, hard coat that will take the row crops and the bramble. Beware of show breeds that live for the beauty contest.

Pound for pound, there is nothing that can hunt better, or give more companionship day after day, than one of these happyscat models. I love the flushers; more importantly, they love everyone they

This is LaighPark Sam, the most beautiful English cocker I've ever seen. Bred by Jim Edgar of Scotland, Sam is owned by Larry Hansen of Prairie Marsh Kennels in Garvin, Minnesota. English cockers (but not all American cockers) are the ultimate vest-pocket pheasant hunters. They'll also produce all upland game and fetch your duck, too. (Photo by Larry Hansen)

hunt for and every bird they seek. If you have the time to hunt – that is, you don't have to run a 440 down the field, turn, and run a 440 back – try one of these little guys. You'll never be sorry.

The Way the Wind Blows

There is nothing more important to a bird hunter than the way the wind blows. That's why I've saved this until last: to bask it in floodlights, hype it up with drumroll, get your attention with a chorus line of long-legged dancing girls.

No matter what type upland gamebird you hunt, you must cast your gun dog into the wind. This ain't the fact with ducks, but that's a later story.

The dog triggers on a bird's scent cone, and the wind must be blowing it to him to register. It stands to reason, as well, that a dog can smell only on the intake, never the outgo. That's why a dog with a clogged nose, or one so tired he could drop, or so hot he's dragging his tongue, is not going to do you much good.

So always work into the wind. Keep your dog cool (water him often), and when his nose is clogged with dust and debris, give him a break and let him mosey about and blow it all out.

Conclusion

Okay, I've worked at game preserves that had 20,000 ringneck and melanistic pheasants in the pens; I've hunted them hard, and I've had thousands brought to hand on the retriever field-trial and test-hunt circuits. But I've never regarded the bird as common. His flair, his grit, his flash, and his wit have always caused my heart to skip a beat. The pheasant is truly king of the farm belt, and he'll never forget it. Once you know him, neither will you.

3

Bobwhite Quail

It's hot. It's noon. You've hunted bobwhite five hours and haven't popped a cap. So you sit in the damp shade of a magnolia tree and call in your dog, whose lolling tongue is flushed pink and dripping. The two of you sit there in this prime habitat and wonder: where are the birds? If you knew what the quail were doing, why they were doing it, and where all this doing was going on, you might fare better on your next bobwhite hunt.

Two in the Bush

To these ends I headed out on the dry, flat prairie, a hundred miles from nowhere, to the bleaks and barrens of Cimmaron land to meet a man who told me over the phone, "I shot two-hundred-fifty wild bobwhites over my two German shorthaired (GSP) pups last year." Two-hundred-fifty bobwhites over two pups that started the season seven months old? In the panhandle of Oklahoma? Where it hasn't rained since the invention of dirt? Where the sun sizzles in the summer and blizzards howl in winter? This is where this guy shot 250 wild quail? While, mind you, Pup and you sit snockered in storied Dixie where the bobwhite harvest is world renowned? Well, be skunked no more my friends. Let's learn the DAY OF THE QUAIL so you know where to hunt, at what time, and for what reason.

Wade Free, Oklahoma state game biologist, appears in the scraped yard of his wildlife refuge home. (We're not all riffraff in this book.

Stick with me and I'll introduce you to a better class of people.) Wade is young, tall, slim, and has the trimmed good looks of a Robert Redford. Same soft brown hair, thin nose—all that stuff. First off, we load his two GSPs in Wade's fat-tired Suburban and tour his refuge. Then we return home. His wife serves tea and cookies while we sit in the shade of his carport and watch his pretty, blonde preschool daughter parade about with a parasol lighted neon-pink by the relentless sun.

Lingo of a Biologist

Wade discounts the drama of his knowledge. He says, "Strictly from a textbook point of view, the day of the quail is a pretty dull matter." I shake my head *ain't so*, and he continues, as only a biologist can talk, "We're basically in the short-grass, high-plains area. What most people actually hunt is the sand-sage grasslands. Zones in this management area are the river bottom, which is typically scattered cottonwood timber, salt cedar, plumb thickets, and skunk brush with a lot of mixed mid- and short-grasses. These include anything from sand bluestem, sideoats gramma, blue gramma, buffalo grass, sand-drop seed, and wheat grass. When you go north out of the river bottom and get up in that hilly country, there are some of the same grasses, but you get more sagebrush."

Once again Bill Koelpin shows us what a gamebird should look like. This is the storied bobwhite. Every bit of Koelpin's structure is hand-carved and painted— even the leaves. (Photo by Mark Deprez)

Bobwhite enthusiast Don Sides of Coffeeville, Mississippi, swings on a flushed bobwhite. Don has built his own hunting preserve: the plowed ground behind him will later be seeded to cover and feed these perky little birds.

Now, mind you, I've hunted Kansas all my life, which is the state north of Oklahoma. It is a known fact that no bobwhites exist west of state highway 81, save for a few who should be in the Larned State Mental Hospital. And here this guy is 200 or so miles west of that highway, and he's finding birds in this dried-out stuff.

Bobwhite: The Dirt Bird

Wade says, "The single thing to remember is that bobwhites are a soil bird." (I'd rather he'd say dirt bird, but he won't. So if you see dirt bird anywhere that's me talking.) "Bare ground not only facilitates feeding, promotes insects, and keeps their feet dry, but it lets the birds move around and have travel lanes and dusting areas. You see, quail spend most of their day walking, scratching, and feeding on the ground. You know they may get through the whole day without having to fly. They are just a fairly open-ground bird."

Wade's black Lab, Jet, joins our English tea party and lays on the cool concrete to eventually sleep and moan. Wade adds to what he's said, "That's why controlled burning is good whether it's on rangeland or in wooded areas; you burn up that leaf litter and expose a lot of native seed and bare ground. Besides burning, we have controlled livestock grazing and strip discing as other management tools to provide bare ground and promote forb production. Forbs (seed-producing plants) are the quail's food source.

"The other thing you must remember is that a quail chick in the spring is an inch or two tall. If you've got a heavy mat of grass, there's no way they can use an area like that. They can't even get over it, let alone feed on it."

The Roost

"Okay," he says, looking about his baked yard, "first thing in the day of the quail is they're going to be on the roost. Generally, they roost in a fairly open area – often, but not always, next to some type of woody cover. They prefer scattered short grasses with fairly open overhead canopy." Note here, my reader, this, then, is where you start your 7 o'clock hunt. Look for this mix of vegetation and bare ground.

A couple of oilmen outside Edmond, Oklahoma, encourage this Brittany to bring them their dinner.

Jim Culbertson of Wichita, Kansas, pioneered bobwhite hunting with Labrador retrievers. He was thirty years ahead of the hunting retriever movement that swept America in the early '80s. Remember, Jim's the owner of Keg of Black Powder featured in the introduction to this book. Jim shoots all upland game with a model 12, full bore, 30-inch barrel. He drops his first quail at 40 yards and his last one at 80.

"They'll leave the roost about daylight. Usually they just walk away; they'll flush only if they were frightened by a predator or something. You may hear the birds talking, for they'll make covey calls and kind of spread out and start feeding. Sometimes they'll feed right in the immediate area; other times, they'll have to walk quite a ways."

Heading for the Groceries

"Food sources a hunter should key in on here would include ragweed, sunflower, gumweed, sand lilly, pigweed, croton, and Illinois bundlefeather," Wade says. Of course, you'll generally not find these plants in Dixie, but I list them *to show how detailed you should be about plants when hunting any gamebird.*

Now let's jump sideways just a minute. I was blessed to know two outstanding quail men: John Bailey of Quail Hills Plantation, Coffeeville, Mississippi, and John Olin, of Nilo Plantation, Albany, Georgia.

Bailey walked his land nearly every day, tossing bicolor lespedeza seeds out through his pinched thumb and index finger—each seed jammed into the soil with the heel of his boot. He had lespedeza on his place 20 feet tall. John swore it was the best quail food God ever put on earth, and that's what you should be hunting in Dixie.

John Olin, who loved Bailey (they compared notes all the time), nevertheless declared, "No, it's yellow corn the bobwhite love," and each day he'd have a wagon go down his interior farm roads strewing corn seed through a propeller on the back. He accomplished two things, he told me. He introduced the right food, and he spread it on an edge where the quail would be feeding.

Now back to Wade. He's saying, "Bobwhites usually stay within a home range of probably less than 40 acres. Several coveys can overlap ranges within that 40 acres, but generally speaking they get most of their life requirements there."

Keeping the Edge

"Now, we all know this about birds," Wade says. "They love an edge. And a typical edge is a transitional zone of two different habitat types.

The late John Bailey of Coffeeville, Mississippi, probably harvested more bobwhite than any other man alive. He owned his own acreage, planted his own feed, and raised his own wild birds. He liked to hang signs on trees where some event occurred; this one commemorates the harvest of his 17,000th quail.

Let's say a soybean field butts up against a hedgerow. That's an edge. I'd concentrate my hunt up to 50 feet from this edge. And remember this, birds can sometimes get edge where you don't necessarily see it at first glance. Consider a pasture with a plum thicket in the middle of it. All the fringe of the thicket would be an edge. Get it?

"And remember this. Our research shows these quail favor 30 to 50 percent bare ground – all day long, all night long. Look for dry, bare ground with a good interspersion of food as well as roosting and escape cover. You need a good diversity of habitat components to reach maximum quail numbers.

"You'll seldom find bobwhites roosted in dense cover. They can't flush and lift and escape through it. So they'll be in short cover, say not more than 6 inches tall."

Back in the Old Days

Let me butt in here. I remember a conversation I had with a quail manager on a large plantation – you'll meet him later – who told me, "We have fewer quail here now than seventy years ago. At that time, there were about 300 tenant families on this plantation. And all those families worked about 5 or 6 acres of cotton, 6 or 8 acres of corn, some sorguhm to grind up for molasses, and a patch of peas.

"They all had a pair of mules to work the crops, a horse to ride to town, and a couple of cows for milk. Well, all the woodlots were fenced up at that time, and that's where this livestock was turned out to eat . . . to keep them out of the cash crops.

"So they ate all the honeysuckle and underbrush – all the scrub stuff coming up. Which made an excellent area for quail propagation. *Woodland suitable for quail is parklike*. Well, that's just about what you have when these horses and cows and mules eat all the foliage they can reach. So, there were more quail here then than there are now."

The description of this wiped-out rural life and consequent habitat mix emphasizes why today's corporate farming with all its homogeneity is so destructive on gamebirds. And, the way everything interworked on the tenant acreage produced a ton of edges? My, o my!

Now, back to Wade, who's still talking: "A covey of quail some days may feed for an hour, and then escape back to what we call loafing cover or woody escape cover for the rest of the day. Other days, they may feed for three or four hours. It has a lot to do not only with weather but also with seed availability and the interspersions of your different habitat components. Sometimes they feed longer simply because of the distance from roost site to food."

Where They Are?

"Now the lesson in all this for a successful hunt is to find areas where you have food, roosting cover, loafing cover, nesting cover, escape cover, and brood cover, plus bare ground in close proximity to all these factors," Wade says.

"Let's take loafing. As I said earlier, quail need a good overhead woody cover (hawk protection) with some bare ground underneath so they can spend most of the day away from predators. And they'll be in there basically loafing around and utilizing the food acquired that morning. Everyone who hunts quail knows that plum thickets and clumps of brush scattered in the right diversity, quantity, and location are the ideal places to put your dog midmorning or midday.

"After quail spend most of the day in there, say at 2 or 3 o'clock in the afternoon, the birds again go back out and feed. They need a full crop when they go to roost. Again, depending upon several factors, they may spend a couple of hours, or the whole afternoon, getting food.

Wade pauses, thinks for a moment, then says, "Essentially, the day of the quail is a day of survival. That bird is going out there, and his main goal is to escape predators and find food. After he's done those two things, his only fear is weather (in order to maintain body temperature). Given bad weather and lots of predators, the quail needs prime woody escape cover to hole up and survive."

What of Water?

"What of water," I ask. "Do quail need standing water?"

Wade smiles and says, "Most research shows quail don't need free-standing water. But they must have water, which they usually get through succulent green plants and insects.

"However, some people who are pretty well known in quail management have indicated that in extremely dry years water on the western fringes of the bobwhite range may be a limiting factor."

Wade goes on talking, but I'll shorthand it for you. *Limiting factor* simply means the water may sustain plants and insects in its vicinity. So, in a drought you should hunt near windmills, ponds, and rivers. Quail do consume free-standing water, but in most cases they are not attracted to water per se, but instead to the microenvironment provided by such water. For this provides the green plants, grasses, and insects (containing moisture) that may not be available on drought-stricken uplands. To us it means when times are dry, hunt wet.

So what have we learned? Everything a gamebird does is related to survival. You are one of those predators he spends his day avoiding. Consequently, to successfully hunt this bird you and your gun dog must outwit the quail at his day's cycle of survival and bring him to gun range.

You do that by always hunting the edge, avoiding high, dense cover, favoring water when available, and concentrating on forbs. These likely places are called, in gun dog parlance, targets of opportunity. That's why you must train your dog in the off-season to recognize these places and go there on his own. Otherwise, you must direct him there by cast, and subsequent whistle and hand signals. Remember, a gun dog hunts, you shoot. He runs, you walk.

Handling Your Gun Dog

The necessity of directing dogs to mixed cover and both linear and upright objectives was proven to me twenty years ago when Delmar Smith, of Edmond, Oklahoma, of gun dog seminar fame, and I took several all-age pointers out on the staked plains of New Mexico and let them go. They blinked their eyes, looked at that endless expanse of nothingness, then made for a windmill 2 miles distant. They could see no other "edge" that would entice a bird.

Momma Quail's Shopping Center

You must always hunt feed plots. Why? In nesting season, momma quail wants to get her peeps to food fast and keep them dry in passage. She fears wet feathers en route as much as a feral cat at home.

Momma quail is quite similar to momma human. They both want their home next door to the shopping center. Momma human would rather take a beating than haul her brood downtown. She wants to get in and out fast, avoid the hassle, and limit the exposure to danger and fatigue.

Momma human's suburban shopping center is a great expanse of concrete. She doesn't walk through tall, wet grass to enter the Piggly Wiggly.

Same with momma quail. Her shopping center is an expanse of bare "dirt," even though it supports sparse vegetation and domed cover. Momma quail wants the dirt to dust not only to keep her brood dry, but to more readily peck at and pick up any seeds that fall from the canopy above.

It stands to reason that as the peep is raised, so shall the juvenile and adult behave. Consequently, it's the purposeless bird hunter who

*The late M. Wayne Willis may be the best gamebird painter America ever pro-
duced. Surely, no one ever painted or carved a quail better than Wayne. As the
American army retreated during the Battle of the Bulge, Wayne was surprised and
surrounded by Germans while he was skinning out a deer he'd just shot: an army
in retreat was no reason for him not to go hunting. (Photo by Chromatech Corp.)*

stalks matted grass, a sea of sedge grass, or a pasture of Bermuda for
quail.

The Bobwhite

Now what are we after? What is this bobwhite quail?

Well, he's a member of the BIG 3. The two biggest field-trial for-
mats in America (pointers and retrievers) are run on mallards, pheasants, and bobwhites. The bobwhite is the star at Ames Plantation,
Grand Junction, Tennessee, each February for the running of the National Bird Dog Championship in which (traditionally) English
pointers and setters vie, and generally pointers win. The pheasants
and mallards appear each year at the fall running of the National Open
Retriever Classic.

The Hand Grenade

You can get an idea of the bobwhite if you have any knowledge of a
World War II fragmentation hand grenade. Put legs, tail, wings, and
head on that grenade, and you've got a bobwhite. Pull the pin on the

thing and let it detonate – and you've got the explosion of this bird when flushed. A covey of bobwhites can make you wet your pants – especially if you're hunting in rattlesnake country. For the bird comes up that fast, and that noisy, and that surprising, and many a gun's been shot straight up in the air by a totally flipped-out hunter.

And why mention rattlesnakes? Am I stretching it? No. Each year Texas is the home of the largest bobwhite harvest in America. You ain't hunted bobwhite until you hunt him on the King ranch. As veteran gun dog trainer and master hunt host Bud Daniel recalls hunting this venue, "I've moved as many as thirty-seven coveys of bobwhites in one afternoon. The other day we stopped by a windmill for lunch. While they were putting the trash in tote sacks, I let two dogs loose. That windmill alone produced eight coveys. And when I say we ran into thirty-seven coveys, you've got to realize we were delayed mightily by the gunners getting off and on the hunting truck."

Little wonder a ton of immortal bird dogs have come out of Texas. They had the birds to train on. Well, you can't be sure you've got a bobwhite quail if all the information you've got is he looks like a fragmentation hand grenade. So let's narrow our field of vision.

A Bird in Hand

The bobwhite is a bird of variegated hues: speckled sedge, fawn, white, and dark and light brown. The distinguishing feature about the

Two stalwarts break tall and tough-going cover to seek bobwhite outside Savannah, Tennessee. The pointer closes his eyes to handle the punishing stuff.

male is a meteor's dash of white that crosses each eye and trails back to the neck. You can see this trail of white when the birds flush – even if there are fifty of them. The hen quail will have the same flash, but it will be buff in color. When the birds come up and you swing to get on them, you'll note the white as you swing past the bird's head. Now you fire to harvest only cocks.

All quail strut. They'd be Jimmy Cagney in real life. The tight, pugged features to the face, the hard-coupled body – small but mighty. Look for these birds in the brush and always expect to see the female appear first. It's that way with most wildlife: the male will usually sacrifice a gal in his harem, or even his wife, to see if any peril awaits him.

Now, this little bird that becomes tame when fed off the back porch will nevertheless leave you standing with an empty magazine. How? Well, he weighs but 6 ounces, is only about 9½ inches long, and flies between 35 and 44 m.p.h.

Their range in North America includes all the eastern seaboard – except for Maine, Vermont, New Hampshire, and most of New York – as far inland as mid-America, plus an extension from Texas on down into Mexico. You'll also find a smattering of them in western Washington and a patch in Oregon.

The Ladies' Bird

Bobwhites are especially adored by ladies. The reason is, this little guy, or gal and her brood, likes to roost close to improvements (that's a Kansas farmer's term for buildings). The birds will be seen walking down the driveway, standing on the pump handle of the water well, pecking in the front yard, and flying past the garden. Their call is always heard coming from a cool glen, and if you stand on the porch and whistle back you'll get an answer.

So it's not likely you'll get through life without some lady charging, "They are so cute. How can you shoot them?"

The answer is, "Lady, I can't. They fly too fast for me."

Another answer is, "If you remove the breast, put it on a char-broiler and leave it there just a flash, then pick it off and eat it with your fingers, you've got something."

Bringing the Quail to Table

Now, I told you above that I had my betters. Jimmy Bryan, long-time manager of the Ames Plantation, home of the National Bird Dog

This no-nonsense hunter has shot for the table and is bringing his bounty home. A German shorthaired pointer, an English pointer, and an Irish setter found in the dog pound have done the job for him.

Championship, and the guy who was telling us about the tenant farmers and their sorghum and mules, recalls that Mr. Ames, from backbay Boston—now surely this would be an epicurean!—had his help hang bobwhites in the basement by strings around their necks. When a quail dropped leaving the head on the string, that's when they cooked them.

Upon telling me this, Jimmy laughed and said, "I think that's one reason it takes so much wine in some of our recipes right now."

For our recipe—and for your delight, kindly throw in with my Southwest heritage—we prepare eight quail to serve four (this recipe enhances all quail discussed later). You'll need ½ cup tequila, ¼ cup lime juice, 3 tbls. olive oil, 1 tsp. ground Mexican oregano, 1 tsp. ground cumin, and 4 hot serrano, pequin, or arbol chilies. Wear rubber gloves when handling chilies.

Flatten the quail by removing the backbone and cracking the breastbone between the counter and your hand. (This applies to all grilled gamebirds; you want the meat to lay flat.) Combine the tequila, lime juice, and 2 tbls. olive oil in a bowl and mix. Smash the chilies, combine with spices, and rub into the birds' skins. Put into a non-metal dish and douse with marinade. Let set for 2 hours.

Just before you place the birds over glowing coals of mesquite embers, rub the quail with that extra tablespoon of olive oil, salt, and pepper. Then place over heat for 4 minutes on each side. Turn one final time and finish off with 3 minutes of exposure.

Serve the quail with a tossed salad, baked potato, and grubstake beans. If you live outside the Southwest, cook with hickory, oak, alder, or any orchard wood. If you have problems finding Southwest ingredients, try the following sources: Armando's Finer Foods, 2627 South Kedzie Street, Chicago, IL 60623, (312)927-6688; Grand Central Market, 317 South Broadway, Los Angeles, CA 90113, (213)624-2378; Johnnie's Grocery, 2030 Larimer Street, Denver, CO 80205, (303)297-0155; Mixtec, 1792 Columbia Road, NW, Washington, D.C. 20009, (202)332-1011.

Hunting Tips Common to All Upland Birds

Now is the time to remember all we learned hunting Mr. Pheasant. We hunt the edges, the seedfields, and those places close to water. Always, we concentrate on finding bare ground with a heavy canopy to protect the lazying bird from hawks—their most dreaded enemy. Yet it is interesting to note what Frances Frazier (the wildlife biologist hired by the late-and-great John Olin of Winchester Arms and Nilo Plantation fame), learned by putting cameras on bobwhite nests at night when all the marauding was going on. The opossum was the biggest culprit. He's the bobwhite's enemy number one.

Points of Objective

Trained bird dogs run to points of objective. We taught Pup that all summer by planting birds where quail will be found during hunting season. Pup remembers this, and when released this is where he goes. Down the borderline between the soybean field and the pine forest, then out into the bares of a pasture to scent a multiflora thicket. Then back through a corn patch and finally along the edge of a bicolor lespedeza patch. Great! He's run every edge and checked every feed plot in sight. That's hunting. If he'd missed something, you'd also have taught him whistle and hand signals during the summer, and you'd have directed him to his oversight.

This is what people never understand; hunting ain't hunting during bird season. The real serious hunting is undertaken in the summer by teaching the dog where to go and what to do. You've also got pen-raised birds planted at these points of objective; so when they come up, you shoot them, and that gives Pup a chance to retrieve. Plus, you hand him the head of the bird as a delicacy. Did you know the original meaning of the word *quarry* (an English term) was entrails given to a dog as a treat?

Don't fear Pup will become hard-mouthed by feeding him bird

parts. That can easily be cured by putting him on the magic table. (See *Problem Gun Dogs*, chapter 6.) For what you've done by so pampering him is made him birdy as hell.

And if your dog don't have the spirit, then all he is a mechanical dog: a pawn to be moved around on a chessboard. That's a horrible thing to follow out hunting. How much better for the dog, when he becomes all-age, to tell you where to go, to figure the land better than you can, to go left for the deadfall when you saw it go right—and always be correct. That's what you get with spirit. The same thing a man gets by hunting: to have faith in yourself.

Casting into the Wind

Now there are some imperatives you should know about hunting all upland gamebirds with Pup. He is always cast into the wind while you sing a song, kind of a constant "Hallllllooooooo," so Pup knows where you are and doesn't have to keep checking back in. You also can outfit Pup with a bell or beeper collar to know exactly where he is.

Anyway, Pup is cast into the wind and eventually hits a bobwhite covey's scent cone. (Every bird gives off an odor. Near the bird the scent cone is only 2 inches wide, but 40 yards downwind, it has spread 20 feet wide.) Pup honors this odor and stops. Then he checks more closely and possibly takes a few stalking steps closer to the bird's site.

You're coming up fast and *silent* from behind. You're not saying, "Whoa boy . . ." and all that nonsense. Why take Pup's attention off the birds he's pointing? You taught him *whoa* last summer; that's the last thing you need to say now.

Also, you walk a wide circle around Pup for several reasons. First, he can now see you and knows exactly what you're doing; second, you've not chanced too close to Pup where you might push back a branch with your body and have it come swinging back in Pup's face, which could make him bird shy; third, no matter where you are when you shoot, your gun's blast will be predicted by Pup, which means the sound will not surprise him and cause him to be gun shy; and fourth, this gives you the opportunity to set up your shot without looking into the sun.

In addition, by walking way around Pup and coming back in, you've now sandwiched the birds between you and the dog. When they come up they're going to be a panoramic theater right in front of his nose. You're going to shoot those heading out at an angle, and Pup will see them fall so he can retrieve deadfall. More importantly, he can now see where the covey lands so he can lead you to birds again.

This is fun. Walking along animatedly, encouraging Pup, "Hunt 'em up Pup . . . dead . . . dead . . . dead. . . ." Then swishing your foot in the grass, moving it about the way you scull a boat with a pole, and making your voice shudder like quail coming up, "BDBDBDBDDBDBDBDBDBDBDBDB." Do it by making a horselaugh with your bottom lip or a rapid flutter of your tongue. Not only does this excite Pup, but it also makes any hidden bobwhite so edgy he finally says, "I can't stand it any longer," and throws caution (and his body) to the wind. There are lots of tricks.

The Edgy Bird

But beware, relocated bobwhites don't always sit tight. You may have Pup on point as you make a circle-walk around him, but the bird won't wait for you—Pup's power won't hold him motionless. Up he comes. Never mind. Fire. For you are not near pup with the *bang*, plus you're never firing in his direction, and both of you can now see this newest deadfall.

When all the singles are accounted for and no new birds have erupted, tap Pup gently behind his head and command, "Hie on." This

The epitome of all gun dogs, an Elhew pointer, is sculpted and cast in bronze by his breeder, Bob Wehle of Midway, Alabama. In sixty years of breeding, Bob has succeeded in creating gun dog athletes, nearly self-trainable, and as beautiful to the eye as a thoroughbred race horse.

is your long searching cast. Pup is using the wind, noting the edges, and striding hard. But you think he may have glossed over a birdy spot, so you hit him with the whistle and command him to stop (which is one long whistle blast). Then you catch up and tell Pup, "Birds, Pup, birds." Then keep telling him, "There are birds in here." But do that only when you are certain this is likely cover. Otherwise, it would be the boy who called wolf one time too often.

The command for Pup to retrieve is, "Fetch it up." Take him by his strong, wide leather collar with welded D-ring, and physically cast him toward the spot where you saw the bird go down. When Pup takes the bird to mouth, hurrah him in, either with your voice or by clapping hands. You also can use a training whistle – one made by Acme called a Thunderer, the big one.

When Pup brings the bird to hand, you should also fondle him. Love him. Let him know he's the greatest. But at the same time, mind you, you're searching for sundry ticks. Heaven forbid either of you gets these killers with their Lyme disease. Okay?

Dog Tired

Water Pup often, and let him rest when either he starts to lag behind you or his tail comes down. A hanging tail is a sure sign Pup's momentum has been lost and he needs a break.

Check his pads often for foreign matter that might have cut a foot or entered between the toenail and the skin. If Pup should break off a toenail, cut the remainder off with your clippers. Otherwise, the half-broken nail will bother him for days. Remember to give water as needed, and let Pup wallow in every mud puddle or creek he finds.

If you're in tall grass or tangles with heavy dust, then wipe Pup's eyes out at every chance. Pour water in them and let the debris pool near the nose. Then flick it away with your handkerchief. Of serious concern is foxtail, spear grass, or anything else that is pointed and barbed. Such things can pierce the body and then migrate – actually traveling completely through the dog. You'll chase it and ring up an expensive vet bill.

Voice and Hand Signals

It's imperative that Pup responds to your voice or hand signal. This is the only way you can keep him from charging out onto an interstate highway or diving into an oilfield sludge pit or some chemical plant's industrial waste. Every time you leave off the hunt and head back to the highway, Pup must wear a leash or check cord so you have total and immediate control.

And remember this: if a dog will come when you call and he'll hold steady upon command, you can shoot birds over him.

Which Gun Dog?

The storied bird dogs for hunting bobwhite quail are the English pointer and English setter. They have dominated the quail championships in America for more than 100 years.

Yet, they do have competition. The Brittany spaniel has won the International Endurance Championship in a three hour heat versus the slicks and the shags in pursuit of bobwhites.

Any of the continental dogs will do you well, except for the English springer spaniel. The springer is just too eager; he lunges to kick up the bird, and he may be beyond your gun's range. Quail just aren't going to hold for a dog that barges through the grass like a Weed Eater. But every statement has its exceptions. I've seen English springer spaniels perform excellently on quail, and even on a more spooky bird, the ruffed grouse. They have the one trait necessary of all gun dogs to hunt bobwhite: they'll bust into any harsh, thorned, or tangled cover to check for birds.

But the German shorthaired, wirehaired, longhaired pointer, or the spinoni from Italy (as another example) will take you bobwhite hunting. And remember, any dog that will come when you ask him to, and whoa when he's found birds, is more than 99 percent of all sportsmen have ever had, no matter his breed!

The Beginning Hunter

The last word: two favored dogs for the starting bobwhite hunter are the wirehaired pointing griffon and the pudelpointer. These dogs can do everything the English pointer can, albeit slower, but they can be more biddable to your mild command. We just don't want to mud-wrestle every time Pup rejects what we're saying. Other fine dogs that can take you bobwhite hunting are the vizsla, weimeraner, small and large Munsterlander pointers, German roughhaired pointer, and any dog that will point. And don't overlook the new hunting red setter.

For every bobwhite I've ever taken while shooting over English pointers and setters, I've taken twenty shooting over hunting retrievers. They are my ultimate hunting dog. No, they don't point, but you learn to read exactly what's happening before them. And you usually

Bird artist supreme, the late M. Wayne Willis, and I hunted the nation's prime bobwhite mecca in southeast Kansas. On very cold mornings we'd find coveys bunched up just like the guys in this painting. (Photo by Chromatech Corp.)

get the bird when it flushes. For more information about hunting quail with retrievers, read any of the books I've written precisely on this subject.

The Preserve Bird

Okay, we've hunted the wild bobwhite. But this is hardly the hunt of the future, what with all the land going corporate, farmers wiping out shelterbelts so the shade of them won't diminish the amount of land to be planted, and the putting up posted signs – not to mention the insecticides, the electric wires, the herbicides, the suburban developments. They are all effective deterrents to keep you and Pup out of the fields. So you go to a preserve and pay to shoot a bird.

Hope your quail aren't on tree limbs. Yes, bobwhites are notorious for this. And why? Because the game breeder and the reserve operator did not put the birds into the correct flight pen. And why not? Simple! Cost lots to build. The pen should be long, wide, and tall.

Rick Smith of Edmond, Oklahoma, ten-time national Brittany championship trainer, housed some quail in a two-story building with a skylight at the top. Sure enough, those birds launched straight toward that one source of daylight. The result? The flushed birds rocketed on launch: they lifted themselves nearly straight up, then set their wings to glide. How different from the general pen-raised bird when released. You know, they sputter up, hit two wing beats, then fall in the grass without landing gear. Any wild bird will fly 40 percent faster than his pen-raised cousin. Anyway, I've been quoted that figure by men who should know. But a bird raised in a tall flight pen can make up some of that speed.

And if you watch them closely you'll see it only takes three seconds to get to full flight. It was early Sunday morning thirty-five years ago when I was driving through Yell Ville (I split the name for emphasis; check your atlas, however, and you'll see it is spelled Yellville) in northwestern Arkansas. Light had just broke when I saw a thin, disheveled man lying in the gutter clutching a crumpled paper sack.

I slid across the seat and yelled out to him, "Hey, pardner! Can you tell me where I could find a town called Yell Ville?"

The old man leaned a bony left elbow on the curb, and with his right hand began studying the stubble of his beard. Then he covered his eyes and looked at me through the slits between the fingers of his fuzzy, orange gloves.

I asked, "Have you ever heard of Yell Ville?" My voice was too loud, but I was getting exasperated.

The old man shook his head in grave doubt.

Then I asked, "What's the name of this place?"

This cock bobwhite is content to sit in the hand of a game preserve operator. Such tame birds make poor hunting if not flight-trained right, but preserve shooting may be the sport of the future.

The man warmed quickly; I'd undoubtedly touched upon his ancient heritage. He dropped a gloved hand from his face, and in toothy smile said, "YU-vul." Which rhymed with shovel.

The point to the story is, the natives might know a Yu-vul bird, but that's not what the guy at the preserve is turning out. Those are domestic-born, imitation-raised substitutes for the real thing. They're Yell Villes, all right. Suitable for a man who doesn't know where he is. Suitable for a man who never in his life shot a full-oxygen-blooded, scat-back, wild-fired bobwhite quail.

The Gun for You

Let's talk about guns. Special guns fit to harvest bobwhite quail. That goose gun, duck gun, pheasant gun, what-have-you, is not really suited. Oh, I know, I've seen men with full-bored corn-shuckers (pump guns to the newly initiated) take my week's lunch money in innocent wagers on quail.

Pick any gun you can shoot well, and go with it. Of course, I'm in love with the ultralight (6 pounds, 4 ounces) Franchi semiauto, 20-gauge, improved cylinder, with 26-inch-barrel, plugged for three shells.

That big Remington was hell on pheasant, but in a bobwhite thicket I could just as well been swinging a 4x10 plank of oak.

Right off the bat with that Franchi, however, I got five bobwhites on the covey rise. A royal flush if you will, which Mr. Shooter with the full-bore Model 12 (remember him; I'll introduce him later) had yet to do that season. And was I in my glory.

The bottom line is to shoot any gun you can handle that feels right, that you can swing easily in tight quarters and reasonably assume you won't hit anything but the bird. Most of us prefer 20 gauges. A few like the 28 gauge. Some try a .410, but that's wrong. The general pattern is pitiful on a .410. And a few gunners still carry the heavy 12 gauge. It's your hunt, so it's your business. Any low-brass light load, say 7½s or 8s will do you well.

One last word to the wise. Never flock shoot. There's more air up there than birds, even though it looks like the sky is jammed with them. It ain't. Pick out one bird, catch him with the swing of your gun, carry through, and fire. That bird you'll hit. Never the flock. Also, a warning, if you will: be sure lead shot is legal for upland game where you're hunting. There are places where it isn't, especially wildlife refuges in the Southwest.

And I admonish you not to shoot a hungry bullet.

Just take what you can use, and leave the rest for the guy, or the generation, behind you.

4

Gambel's Quail

*For the past seventeen years Gambel's have frequently caught me cooking on my outdoor grill as they fly in before dusk, plopping into a piñon tree, preparing to roost there, calling late arrivals with a comical four-count **goink**. It sounds like someone pumping a hand-held oil can. And the birds rustle up there as they settle, hoping no one comes close by in the dark. For if they do, the birds are compelled to fly, and that's bad because they don't see well at night.*

TATTERED CLOUDS LIKE shreds of some flag of truce raised long ago by a cavalry troop take the wind above us. We hunt Gambel's quail under the thin, white banner on legend-filled Indian lands – these great sloping fields of strewn lava racks, of thorn trees, and steep-pitched arroyos near my home of Sedona, Arizona.

I watch Bill Parton and his four-year-old Llewellyn setter move effortlessly before me. He and the dog are hunters. Bona fide hunters; not opening-day hunters, nor outdoor-catalog hunters, nor two-martini story-telling hunters.

In the town of Oracle, Arizona, Parton makes his living as a hunting guide, carver, and sculptor. He lives anywhere there ain't a clock connected to it: he must have time. Time to ambush the elk, call the turkey, intersect the deer, surprise the javelina, set the quail.

A Gambel's cock (left) and hen are caught foraging beneath a saguaro cactus in the Sonoran desert. (Photo by Bill Parton)

In everything he is thorough, neat, and complete. He asked to use my band saw the other day and brought his wife's vacuum sweeper to clean up. I like Bill Parton.

The Gambel's Nature

He says, "You can always have a fifteen-bird limit on Gambel's, for they're hard little buggers to find when they don't want to be found. If you take and shoot up a covey once, you'll seldom have the option again. You're generally getting into juvenile birds, and that first baptismal by fire will convince them to shun you ever more." And yes, folks, Bill also tells a good tale.

We take a few more steps and the setter, Bandito, makes game, starting her set tentatively. But now she locks and five birds loft. Bill fires and two cocks fall, Bandito fetches them up, and I take one to hand. He's a beautiful bird, but unlike the Mearns quail (coming up next) he thrills you daily as you sight him. (The Mearns is a true wilderness bird, staying as far from man as he can.)

I see a Gambel's cock in the summer from my window, always taking the shadows to disappear, always tending his brood. In the outdoors, the Gambel's cock may be the best of all fathers. Bachelors have been known to lure away clutches to raise themselves. There's just some instinct in them. They are easy to find; they have a diminutive call they use to announce location. It is repeated throughout the day. And it has a cozy effect, letting you know civilization is right out the door, but there's also a wildness there.

At night they issue a three- or four-part call that goes *bomp beep bomp bomp.* (Bird calls were never meant to be written down.)

Why Quail Reproduce

Parton says, "They've done research here in Arizona and found that the amount of vitamin A in a bird's liver determines next year's hatch. This is a poor year; we should have had fifty birds in that covey instead of five. The amount of vitamin A depends on rains that fall from October through March. The rains make the green seeds grow, and the birds can eat well early (Gambel's are 90 percent vegetarian). That gears up their reproductive systems, and they pair off and hatch. But scant rains . . . scant hatch."

"With or without birds," I tell him, "It's good to be out."

"Oh, we may get into birds," he says. "There's a way to work Gambel's. Let's say we bump birds. The thing to do is fire, fetch, then sit down in that exact spot and wait. No need chasing the fleeing quail. That's their game, and you'll seldom catch them. They run and veer at right angles, they have all sorts of tricks."

No Place to Run

Parton continues, "But each busting covey has a staging area, a place

It's a hot hunt for Gambel's quail so Bill "Web" Parton of Oracle, Arizona, calls in his brace of English setters and gives them a drink. I've seen Parton tote as many as 8 quarts of water on his cartridge belt. That, folks, is 16 pounds of weight.

they go when they've flown and run and dodged and all. You sit and wait for the calls. Wait twenty minutes. Then you cast your dog in that direction, and when you get a point, be ready. You'll have scattered singles and doubles, and they'll fly. They won't run. You know why? *Because they have nowhere else to go.* This was their hideout and you found it. They're doomed. So they sit tight, like a bobwhite, and await their fate."

"I know they are very territorial," I tell him.

"It's the truth," he says, "You see that swale down there?" He points. "Well, I've jumped four coveys in there, and each time they've regrouped on that saddle up there."

We hunt Gambel's quail 'til noon, then double-back to the pickup, to sit on the tailgate and eat pudding from aluminum tins. I lean my Franchi against the tailgate, Parton balances his 20-gauge, over-and-under Browning on his lap. He says, "Come on, I'll show you something."

We take our guns and start climbing. It doesn't look good; there are spent shells everywhere. "The place has been shot up," I tell him.

"Yeah, but there's something else I want you to see."

We top a hill to be confronted with redrock outcroppings on a bluff. We turn left, going down through a gradual valley, then we climb again. "There," he says. I look in the distance at the caved-in ruins of some Indian village. When we finally get there, I see *manos* and *metates* and pottery shards scattered about. No one's raided this place.

A Redrock Lesson

"See that?" says Parton, pointing at a *metate* with his toe. "The Indians busted it when they left. They figured everything had a spirit in it, and when they were no longer going to use it to grind corn, they busted it to release the spirit."

I stand on the hill, the wind brushing my cheek, and look at the great gorge before me. Down there will be the creek where they fetched water. Gambel's quail call in the distance. Off to the left, I see the field the Indians cleared: there's not a rock on it. It is one more ultimate hunt for me. The kind I love so much. Gamebirds lead me both to nature and to the nature of things; they help me to see clearly today what I would have missed yesterday; and they help me to find affirmation in my choice to leave civilization. I'm not interested in making money, but memories. I seek not fame but, instead, familiarity with little things.

We depart the ruins under the law of present-day wilderness trails – "Leave only footsteps, take only memories" – and hunt back to

Parton's English setter points a covey of Gambel's behind a prickly pear cactus.

the pickup. There are no birds. Parton says, "Another advantage of winter rains is you get thick cover. Birds are more prone to set then, not so inclined to run."

"Well, this cover is nothing," I say.

"But next year it could be thick and birds everywhere – if we get the rains. Nothing can reproduce itself like Gambel's quail."

Yields of the Past

"I know," I tell him. "In 1932, Jack O'Connor, one of America's truly great hunting journalists, wrote that he saw 10,000 Gambel's quail in one day. And he also mentioned a Judge Richard E. Sloan, who wrote in his own book, *Memories of an Arizona Judge*, that from one desert station on the Southern Pacific Railroad, 35,000 dozen quail were shipped to market in one year by market gunners and trappers."

"Hunting won't wipe them out," says Parton. "Our fish and game people have conducted experiments on that, putting one hunted plot next to another that's not hunted. At the end of the season, the two plots, have relatively the same number of birds."

"How's that?" I ask.

"Because nature is the great killer of Gambel's quail. The hunters' harvest is nothing compared to nature's culling. If there's a great hatch in the two plots, then lots of hunters come and take birds, but never to a percentage where it is noticeable. Yet, if the hatch is down in both plots, the hunters get discouraged and don't come back. It's the law of diminishing returns. Hunting pressure always corresponds to the Gambel's population."

I say nothing to Parton, for I happen to know he thinks like I do: you don't need a bird to hunt. To hunt is not to kill a bird, but to find yourself and the world you live in.

Miles to Go

It's getting dark now; soon the birds will sail to the piñon trees to roost for the night, calling as they land there, giving that rolling two-tone call. And they'll rustle about, changing places.

We drive home, my mind's eye seeing the sweep of the liver-ticked-and-white English setter making gull swoops on a far rise, feeling the wind on my face as I toe a broken *metate*, recalling the musings of Parton as he tells of this thing or that, smiling at the surprise of stumbling onto a Christmas cactus with its fragile red blossoms.

We drive home, down through lush, green canyons with rushing brook water and tall, thick trees you'd never imagine could be found in

Many desert hunters prefer German wirehaired pointers for upland game dogs. They have a matt of protective hair to ward off cactus and wait-a-bit bushes.

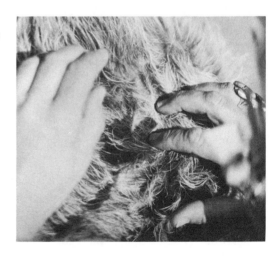

a desert. I think of the lost ones, the Indians who passed before us. How they must have loved this place. How they must have hated to leave it. I know that's how we feel: me and Parton and a dog named Bandito.

In Closing

The same guns, shells, gun dogs, hunting attire, and hunting and cooking methods that work for bobwhites will work for Gambel's as well. However, in the years that I've lived in the Sonoran desert, I have noticed the dog of preference is the German shorthaired or wirehaired pointer. Many prefer the latter because his dense coat guards against cactus. The former? I just don't know. I've asked many and they can't say. It's just the dog they chose.

The Gambel's quail cock is a gray bird with black mask, brown cap, and long tilted-forward black plume. He has brown and white racing stripes on his sides, and a gray back with fawn breast and a black tarantula (or something that looks like that to me) on his belly. The female has the plume, the racing stripes, and the gray body. As always, she must be the color of dirt. The young, like all quail, will scoot along like rolling golf balls. For that's how big they are, and how fast they run.

Gambel's quail are our first desert bird, occurring principally in Arizona and New Mexico. They're neither small nor large, but just big enough to make a meal—weighing an average of 6½ ounces and measuring 10 to 11 inches from bill tip through tail. They scoot aloft at 40 m.p.h., and can run 15 m.p.h. But they prefer to walk, and it is a delight to see both parents heading a trail of peeps. They stop and scratch vigorously at the sandy soil, and the young ones seem to know everything they'll ever learn by the time they're the size of a baseball.

The Gambel's is a pert, jolly, lovable bird that will keep you company morning and night. I've never met anyone who didn't love the Gambel's quail. Oh yes, Gambel was an army surgeon and amateur ornithologist. He had his likes in Mearns, the "discoverer" of Mearns quail—coming up.

5

Mearns Quail

*Mearns quail are a national treasure. They are that lovely,
that scarce, and that revered. And they are that doomed.
Though they live on insects in the summer, in the winter
they prefer the nuts of nut grass, even though they supple-
ment their diet eating leaves, roots, and berries. The federal government has a policy of leasing forest land to
cattlemen whose herds denude the range and trample out
the nut grass. If we don't change our range policy, it's
adios for this jaunty bird, who will be cast into whim's
way in the daffy game-management policies of Mexico.
(There are experts who do not agree with me. See the top
Mearns quail authority of our time: David E. Brown,*
Arizona Game Birds, *University of Arizona Press, Tucson, Arizona.)*

THE MEARNS QUAIL is the bird hunter's feathered grail. We know where
he lives. We know how to harvest him. But when knocking on this
delightful fellow's door we'll not be taking the legal limit. We'll take but
one or two each as a total for a two-day outing. That's how precious we
judge this impeccable bird and his demure lady of the high chaparral.
Plus, the scenery where he lives and the high-altitude air are both so
beautiful and invigorating you can heartily spend a summer vacation-
ing here.

The most magnificent gamebird photo I've ever seen—a perfectly symmetrical covey of Mearns quail looking like puppies snuggled in a litter box—was shot under a dog's point. Such a shot surely will never be duplicated. (Photo by Fred Belman)

There is much to know and appreciate about the Mearns. He is the desert's bobwhite: nearly equal in size and scat and mystique and taste. Unlike his neighbors—the scaled quail and Gambel's—the Mearns quail does not run from a dog's point, nor flop into a snake hole. No, he's up and at 'em—hitting the air with all the thunder and speed of the bobwhite, startling Pup, running chills up the hunters' legs, ducking behind a cat-claw mesquite—knowing all the tactics his Dixie counterpart has perfected.

He's No Bobwhite

He differs in one very important respect from the dirt-loving bobwhite. The Mearns must have grass, abundant grass, tall as a man's knee (but always in a live oak setting, never grass for grass's sake). Living that submersed in cover, the bird will hold for a point, thinking the dog will move on. But if not, then this depth prompts the startling, erupting flushes . . . the birds flying to taller grass, which makes for meticulous kicking out of the singles.

Unique to this quail, he's round. At least, his fluffed plumage makes him appear round, like a feathered softball with a tip of a tail coming out one side (the shortest tail in quaildom) and a pug-billed head protruding from the other.

And with that, most similarities cease between the two species. For the bobwhite tolerates man, while the Mearns can't stand him. The Mearns seeks haunts far from improvements, deep in his live oak park. And where the bobwhite thrives on domesticated row crops, the Mearns scratches the wild for his living. Digs his dinner out of the dirt, he does. So to do that, he has nails like a Chinese princess. It's a fact. That's another of the unique determinants of this bird: blue legs and claws with "fingers" so long he can't clutch a tree limb. This bird cannot perch; he roosts like the bobwhite, in a tail-end circle, on the ground.

The bird weighs 8 ounces, and is some 8 inches long. He lives in the live oak country of Arizona, New Mexico, and Texas along the Mexican border at an average elevation around 5,000 feet. These quail hide before a dog and will flush only at the last moment. Once flushed, they'll fly and sail up to 300 yards. This means, then, you must have a dog rock-steady to wing and shot. The birds flush, you fire, Pup freezes, you yell, "Hup" (for him to watch), he sees the birds relocate, you tap him on the back of his neck and tell him, "All right" (which means to relocate), and you flush the spread-out covey again as singles. No way can you have a breaking, barge-in dog that will chase these birds, barking, and never let them stop short. Never. Incidentally, Mearns flight and running speeds are not as fast as the Gambel's quail.

The Mearns is also called a harlequin (which means clown) quail because of its dramatic plumage. I rate it and the capercaillie of Europe as the two most precious gamebirds I've ever encountered.

Cock of the Walk

The male is one of our most beautiful birds: black-and-white streaked head, a russet crest (like an ill-fitting toupee), a buff-flecked, brown back, and mahogany belly. The female has a customary drab and demure camo coloring of cinnamon, with brown, black, and buff markings.

I feel the Mearns live as a family unit – they don't seem to inter-mingle with their neighbors. That's why hunters say, "You'll not get full plumage in a Mearns, for you're always shooting this year's birds." If you're a seasoned sportsman, however, you can pick out the old cock (same as the bobwhite) when he flies off; you'll see the brilliant white flashes of his head. The old sage is usually last to loft. He employs the same tactic big bucks use when pushing does before them in a clearing.

Who Killed Roger Mearns?

The gun is not the Mearns' nemesis. The bird nests and roosts on the ground. (The hen digs a hole for her brood and mats a hinged door from grass for concealment.) Should cattle, for example, eat the Mearns' cover, then the birds can be immediately wiped out by Cooper's and sharp-shinned hawks, night-stalking skunks, coyotes, and ringtail cats. Also, the bird's diet is favored by both wild and domesticated animals: thus they must live in a very competitive world.

The bird's nature also works against it. Mearns have a minimal foraging range and are reluctant to leave it. Consequently, you can usually find the same covey in the same spot at the same time day after day. It's not unusual to flush a covey, shoot, then look down and find a spent shell from a previous hunter.

A Bona Fide Hunt

There are three of us on this trip. Bill Berlat is a Tucson lawyer/sportsman; this is his territory. Jim Pettijohn is a retired TWA pilot and bird carver who has won Best of Show, amateur division, in decorative life-size bird-carving at the Ward Brothers Foundation World Championship in Ocean City, Maryland. Jim seeks a bird so he can carve a wood counterfeit. I'm along for ballast.

We stop in a lovely draw called Fish Canyon when Berlat releases the tidy German shorthaired pointer bitch called Shadow. She spins and dumps and squints at the bright morning sunlight. (It is January, the nation's freezing, but it's jacket weather here). We're parked in gently rolling high-grass country with good stands of live oak and mature manzanita. There's no cactus here; just an occasional prickly pear and a rare cholla.

From past experience, we know the birds will be scratching about for nuts, tubers, larvae, or insects in dark, damp earth beneath the shade of live oaks. And they'll be on the flats or in the bottoms of draws. So the plan is to work up one draw, cross over the crown, and come back down the other.

Dogwork

Immediately, the shorthair makes contact. But she's catching old scent; the birds were here earlier. Now she runs low-headed, trailing track. Suddenly, she has their scent full-bore. Jim Pettijohn enters the scent cone carrying a camouflaged Ithaca 12-gauge pump (it's his turkey gun), and the birds explode.

"There they go," shouts Berlat, lifting his side-by-side 28-gauge AyA. The guns are popping. But the birds know this game better than the hunters. They fly toward both men. And no one can fire, for the

Ever see a prettier face? This is Brandy, a Brittany that specializes in Mearns.

target includes both bird feather and human flesh. We laugh at being outwitted, pick up the one bird down, walk on west, and enter another draw. But we stop en route to water Shadow. That's necessary when hunting a dog in desert country. Water Pup often at the start of a hunt, and he'll run cool all day. But let him boil over – like a car's radiator – and you'll sit in the ditch a spell before the dog can run again.

Also, this is sandbur country, and you need to call your dog in when it goes lame. Take your pocket comb and flip out the burrs. Look between the toes. Make sure each paw is clean. If your dog's a tenderfoot, then outfit him with rubber boots.

Some men hunt Mearns by looking for fresh diggings – a series of holes about 2 inches long, 1 inch across, and 2 or 3 inches deep – and then call in their dogs to track 'em out. Others may not want their dogs tracking foot scent; they prefer horizon-busting rangers who barge to wind, button-hook scent, then leap back to sock it to them. In either case, the Mearns will generally hold till the hunter arrives.

I always regard live oaks as targets of opportunity, so I check each one – especially those that grow at the shoulder of the hill where the hillside angles onto the meadow floor.

I suppose 90 percent of all coveys are located under live oak, digging in damp ground, on the shade side of the tree. That's not science talking, that's just me.

Roughing It

We've hunted the morning, and the sun is high when Pettijohn takes a short rack of ribs from the cooler and places them, wrapped in aluminum foil, against the pickup's hot manifold. Soon we sit in canvas chairs and eat hot ribs sludged with Jim's secret sauce. Plus, there's a scoop of deli slaw to go with it. For bread, we drag tortilla chips through a nacho-cheese dip. Quite frankly, one does well in the high Sonora.

Folding up camp and winding out of the canyon, Berlat pulls off a side road and takes us to Santa Rita Abbey. We enter to find the monastic sisters at noon prayer. They pray in song, and their voices come clear and bright, soft and loving. I have never heard anything so beautiful: I sit in a pew and feel I've walked from the desert under a waterfall.

Down the road from the abbey and in sharp contrast to all that it stands for, we pass the Cowboy Bar and Steakhouse (or some name like that) at Sonoita. This place will rumble Saturday night. But without us. We're going down the road to Patagonia where the visitor can eat at the Feed Lot restaurant, wet his throat at the Last Gasp saloon, and sleep in the Stage Stop Inn.

The Mexican Connection

But it's too early to check in. We drop our duffel and head for the Mexican border, passing a house Berlat's been checking for years. He tells us in advance, "There'll be an old man sitting on the porch in the sun." We round the bend and look back to see: there he sits! Berlat tells us, "Come by a hundred years from now and he'll still be sitting there."

I tell Bill and Jim, "He's a retired gun dog writer."

Later, we're stopped back in the hills by a National Guard jeep. The driver asks us, "Where are we?" And Bill and Jim and I must look at each other and try to keep from laughing. "I'll sleep better tonight knowing they're out here," I offer.

But that seems to be the way it is with a Mearns hunt. It's always fun and festive, free and easy. Never have I had more memorable outings for game anywhere on earth.

This Man Mearns

In my mind's eye I see the gold miners, 100 years ago, bringing their diggings down out of the crevices in these hills. They are a weary, gaunt outfit. Dead in more ways than one. I then recall that chance day I entered Aaron Cohen's Guidon bookstore in Scottsdale, Arizona, and casually mentioned Mearns. If I had not, to this day I wouldn't know who Mearns was. Aaron stands, walks to a shelf, pulls out a book, blows the dust from the top, and hands it to me, saying, "Mearns is in here." I couldn't believe it. I'd hunted for the man harder than I'd hunted for the bird named after him.

I looked at the book, *Ornithologists of the United States Army Medical Corps,* by Edgar E. Hume, the John Hopkins Press, 1942. I bought the book and left, thanking all the gods of the hunt that I'd finally broken the Mearns conspiracy: I happened to chance upon a non-bird hunter who let me break through on the mystery bird. I speed-read the pages, learning in short order that Mearns was a miraculous surgeon, sportsman, and zoologist. Why, he accompanied President Theodore Roosevelt on his African safari and is noted in the resultant book, *African Game Trails,* as ". . . the best shot in the party." Mearns took 3,000 birds on the expedition, shooting most of them with a rifle, a Winchester .30-40.

Starting his Army medical career at Camp Verde, Arizona, during the Apache encounters (1884–88) the 5-foot 4-inch, 140-pound, Highland Falls, New York, native gathered flora and fauna for the Smithsonian Institution. While there and during subsequent assignments, bird hunter supreme Lieutenant Colonel Mearns once shot a green parrot (with his rifle, as usual) while on campaign against the fierce Moro in the Philippines. It is said, "His nonchalant . . . clambering over the fence of a Moro compound to find the precious specimen in the full and temporarily undisputed possession of a reluctant armed Moro . . . appalled the hardy campaigners who had seen men die violently for infinitely less provocation."

It was simple: Mearns wanted his parrot.

It was simple: the Moro handed it to him.

The book on Mearns ends by saying, ". . . (his) zoological additions to the national collections number approximately: mammals 7,000; birds, 20,000; reptiles, 5,000; fishes, 5,000."

Gambel was equally productive. (Remember his quail?) Look him up.

Adios

Well, we've intruded on this *trofeo de la chaparral alto* long enough. Recluse that the bird is, if he were armed he should have shot us.

But alas, I must part with the truth. As I climb in the pickup, a chilled wind begins to rise in the canyon and we turn on the headlights so the dashboard lights glow neon-blue. I say beneath my breath, *"Adios Amigos,* that's just the way it is. There are no permanent tenants in the Sonoran desert if you've got a herd of cattle stamping out your house and home."

Two miles down the road we stop and clean our birds in a running stream. I will cook mine tomorrow the same way I do bobwhite.

Once again, you use the same gun, shell, hunting attire, and gun dog as you would for Gambel's quail. Mearns cocks are an incredibly dramatic bird some 9½ inches long. They weigh 7 ounces, and sport a black head with intricate striping and a tan crest that drapes back. The belly is gray to olive brown, extensively spotted with buff, white, and black markings. The sides and flanks are gray with dots of white, cinnamon, or brown. The breast is solid brown. The hen is a faded male, the predominant color being brown.

The distinguishing characteristic of this quail you can't see. That's the steel-belted pelvic drive muscles (like the English pointer) the bird must use to extract his food from the earth.

Mearns quail are like the special gal in your life. You go out with all the rest, but this is the one you take home to marry.

6

Scaled Quail

> *The scaled quail lives in a desolate expanse of cactus,*
> *thorn trees, kerosene grass, and greasewood flats. I thank*
> *God for putting this pretty little bird out there to give such*
> *country a gentility and beauty and provide the men and*
> *women who live there a day of sport.*

THE SCALED QUAIL looks like one of those great carp you see in decorative Japanese pools. That's right. Each feather on the bird's body looks like a great big carp scale. But they are a beautiful color. Each one is an iridescent tone of gray-blue: both male and female. You can tell the sexes apart, but not on the covey rise, unless you're a very good color decoder. Like sighting the clear buff on a male's throat. That white topknot won't help you: both sexes have it, which is why the bird got the moniker "cotton top."

These birds frequent the same states as Mearns quail. However, they occupy a broader range of old Mexico.

They are larger than Gambel's quail, weighing about 7 ounces (male) and 6 ounces (female).

New Mexico

I've hunted these birds mostly in New Mexico, and when it comes to the part of the state where the birds hang out, what can you say? What with the greasewood flats, the wind-piled sand dunes, and the primary horizon-breaker a juniper bush. There's some irrigation in this country, so you hunt the watered fields, plus all the tailing ponds and the tanks (that's a pond to eastern folk).

Other than that, you just walk the expanses, hour after hour, mile after mile, hoping your dog lifts something. It's not so bad in Arizona or Texas where you have overlapping bird ranges: you can get a bob-white with a scaly in Texas, or a Gambel's or even a Mearns in Arizona. But in New Mexico, you're stuck with scalies or you can carry a rifle for antelope.

Better yet, you can hunt the old stomping grounds of Ben Lilly, the world's greatest mountain lion hunter, and poke around the San Francisco River area near Springerville, Arizona, in the northeast mountains of that state. There, you'll also mosey into the range of blue grouse, turkeys, and, surprisingly, Mearns.

Don't think I'm a critic of New Mexico. Quite the opposite: I love it. Sure, there are the bares, but if you want to see the most beautiful country in the world, go to Cumbres. It's like God got up and watered

This cocky scaled quail struts before a rock and a dried-out limb. Seldom will you get close enough to this bird to take a photo. (Photo by Bill Parton)

and swept it every morning. Take the Chamas and Toltec scenic railroad ride in the spring and summer. Fish anytime. When you die, have a buddy sneak you up there and bury you in a national forest. That would be living!

When I hunt scaled quail, I carry my old Remington 12-gauge model ll00 with the long barrel and the modified choke. I want to be able to reach for these birds: they can flush too far to front. They just have a hair trigger about them. And why not? What vegetation do they have that will dependably shield them? Mighty little. I just forget about hunting out singles. No telling where they go. Oh yes, I shoot 7$^{1}/_{2}$s.

There's Always a Reason

There's a reason I hunt the bleaks and the bares for this delightful scaled (or blue) quail. You'll recall up front in this book I described hunting: it is not to kill, it is to live. It is to learn life and revere life. It is to enjoy life and to make life more secure for the total population of the game you hunt, and yourself.

So why New Mexico – the worst part? I have a hunting friend there. He is B. J. Pierce, three-time World Champion calf roper in the early 1950s. And John, his son, is my godson. One does not hunt for game alone.

But here comes Bill Parton again. You'll recall we met him hunting Gambel's quail. Bill is a sensitive, thoughtful, discerning guy who is also a master hunter. You'll also recall I measure a hunter by how well he wears his mud. In this case, it's how well Bill Parton wears his dust and his sweat.

In the world of dirt, he's a fashion statement.

Parton hunts the Oracle Junction area of Arizona – a high plateau broken up with repeated washes predominated by mesquite. Plus, there is yucca there. The washes define the resultant soft-grass hills. So it is hill and wash, hill and wash.

Using the Land

"Watch the topography of the land," says Parton. "If I push the scaled quail into a wash bank, or into heavy prickly pear, or a line of this mesquite, the bird will tend to hold. This works best with scalies when you're on edge-country where the described conditions exist.

"But most of the time I find scalies in very open grass. And no matter where you locate them, in my experience, scaled quail coveys tend to jump wilder and run from where you mark them down.

You never know what's going to happen on a bird hunt. I was idling under a tree when my partner flushed a covey; one bird bent off and glided to land directly above my head. I harvested him with film.

"The really neat thing about the scalie," Parton says with an admirer's laugh, "is they loft when they flush. A Gambel's will come out very low and hug the ground like a radar-guided missile. Typically, they'll aim for a bush or something. But scalies loft up like a pheasant, and then go out so that in shooting I wait until they hit the top until I fire. This practice of lofting, I must admit, does make the scalies more vulnerable than Gambel's quail.

"Another thing. I shoot over pointing dogs." Bill Parton is a Llewellyn setter fancier and always tends a kennel of them, except for that one rare purchase where I talked him, somehow, into buying a Chesapeake Bay retriever. That was the day.

But anyway, Parton says, "Because of the pointing dogs, I shoot a very open-choked double gun. Now, the average guy will take long shots because his dogs are knocking the birds up. But I tend to lose them when I try this. It's better to just bust the covey and not even fire

a shot. Then watch the birds down and go point each single you want
to take."

Where the Game Is

"Another interesting thing about scalies here," adds Parton, "is we have
sky-island country. That is, the plateau is flat but right there, like "Up
Jumped Mary," a mountain zooms into the sky. We call them sky is-
lands. And what that permits the hunter to do is hunt from the arid
desert floor clear up to the subalpine zone.

"Now, on the mountains the dogs seem to find the scalies on the
bottom of the ridges, but out on the flat, the birds will be just on the
flat. Follow me? When the birds move up against a mountain, the
dogs'll work the bottom of the deeper canyons. Invariably they'll be in
teddy bear cholla."

(Note: if you don't know cholla, don't ever introduce yourself. It's
that small, spindly, crazy-armed cactus of 10 billion soft thorns. The

*M. Wayne Willis painted these scalies for a Kansas cattleman. Wayne generally
hated commissions; they limited his artistic discretions. One patron, at the unveil-
ing of a painting of his favorite quail haunt, gasped and cursed, "That ain't where
that cottonwood tree stands." Wayne rose up in a huff to scornfully entone to the
man, "God didn't know where to plant the trees." (Photo by Chromatech Corp.)*

This is the way to hunt scalies: a good horse, a long-range pointer, and a going-away shot as the birds flush.

things can seemingly penetrate a Vibram sole. And a myth among Arizonans is that cholla can leap. Okay, back to Parton.)

"The reason the birds'll be in this cholla," he explains, "is the dogs can't push them out of this wicked stuff." Amen.

"Don't let anyone tell you scaled quail can't be hunted effectively with a pointing dog. It just takes a very specialized individual to hunt desert quail. But to do that, and here's the catch, the hunter has to throw out the notion that it isn't okay for a dog to break point and relocate on his own. In other words, the handler must turn the hunt over to his dog; he must trust the natural hunting instincts of his dog. Bill Parton and Mike Gould, who you'll meet later, both believe in dogs that self-hunt; in dogs having total field authority and initiative.

"I have two setters that hunt together," says Parton. "And one will lock up within the scent cone, while the other will go out and come around from the other side and stop the birds from running. That's a desert quail hunting duo."

Another Cook

Not only is Parton a master hunter, but he knows how to cook as well. He crock-pots the whole plucked-and-cleaned bird for about three hours. Then he shreds the meat and puts it in tamales, tacos, and barbecues. He'll also steam some and shred it to put into salads. Bill says, "We eat a lot of quail. Shredding the meat permits us to have a great variety of dishes."

Remember, scaled quail are a table delicacy, and one is blessed when he learns how to not only bring them to the bag, but from the bag to the table.

7

California Quail

This is a bird that flocks together, loving each other and man. They may be found in city parks, front yards, and down by the garden where the irrigation canal runs through. It is incredible for an old bobwhite hunter who thought a large covey rise was 50 birds to one day flush 500 California quail in one tumultuous explosion.

YES, THE BIRD of bounty, of togetherness, and of availability. If you have water, you'll find this bird congregated. A creek bank, an irrigation canal the bird can handle (no steep concrete sides), or a borrow ditch of water. Anywhere there's a puddle.

The California quail (locally called the valley quail) is a bright and flashy guy, and gal, just like their Gambel's cousin. Once again, both sexes are plumed (the female's topknot is brown, the male's black). The male bears bold face markings of black and white, with a dark brown skullcap inscribed in a white border; the female is a faded, subdued version of the male. Both sexes display one totally telltale identification: they have scaled feathers on their midchests and bellies.

This is another 7-ounce quail, some 10 or so inches long, and it can really scoot when airborne—about 40 m.p.h. when cruising, topping out near 60 m.p.h. when gunned.

When apart from water, you'll find these quail hiding out in open woodlands, brush-tangled creek bottoms, classic chaparral, grassy slopes, windblown stacks of brush, canyon rims, grainfields, and vineyards.

Bill Koelpin gives us his rendition of a pair of California quail, and does he give it good. (Photo by Mark Deprez)

Habitat

Knowledgeable hunters learn to cast their dogs to California quail by recognizing their favorite food sources. These are many, including deervetch, fillare, mimoso, forbes, bur clover, lupin, ocotillo, manzanita, elder, mountain rye, and snowberry. California quail also like serviceberry, hackberry, gooseberry, sage, mesquite beans, and cultivated crops like alfalfa. They may also be found scratching under your house bird feeder or in your ornamental prickly pear.

California quail ranges from lower Baja California through Washington and inland some to Idaho and Nevada. It nests in grass on the ground, roosts on limbs, rises to eat and drink, and then, like the bobwhite, seeks shelter to loaf, dust, and snooze. Not every tree or bush will do, however; the main requirement is dense foliage to screen the friendly bird from detection while roosting. Yet unlike its Gambel's cousins, these California quail avoid thick chaparral and dense woodlands.

The Gourmet's Bird

This is probably your epicurean quail, since its intake is estimated to be 95 to 97 percent vegetarian. I prepare mine by splitting the quail down the back and wrapping the breast with salt pork or bacon, using toothpicks to keep it together. I broil about fifteen minutes on a hot grill, and salt and pepper to taste. I love to eat California quail with okra pickled in chilies.

A Sporty Bird

Hunters prize this bird for its sportiness. You get a hefty covey rise, an explosive flight mixed with evasion tactics, and touch-and-go landings – the birds hit running only to launch again if pushed. A pointing dog can work them good, if he does not crowd them. As with ruffed grouse, the dog must stop his forward progress immediately upon detecting the covey's scent cone.

The bird can also be taken with well-trained Labrador retrievers cast far about the birds and whistled back in to block them. The Labs also can push the birds back toward the waiting or advancing gun.

The Gun to Use

Since you will get distant covey rises, a gun with a modified choke is usually carried. Shell of choice is usually the No. 7½, but heavier shot is the next selection because of distance and diminishing lack of shot impact.

I've always hunted these birds with a 12-gauge Browning over-and-under because of its balance. It carries, rises, and swings well. Second gun of choice is the standby Remington 1100.

But that's not to say you can't get into these birds with the 20 gauge, because you can. And there's just something about the thin gun: a smaller gauge can be a delicacy, a refinement, and a rise to a higher pursuit.

The Dog of Choice

There is not a gun dog I could not take for California quail. The flushers can lift them, the retrievers can block them, and the bird dogs can point them. Versatile hunting dogs imported from mainland Europe are very popular on the West Coast. You'll find many German shorthaired pointers after California quail. The Wirehaired pointing griffon, pudelpointer, weimeraner, visla, Brittany, and their cousins are all popular, as are the traditional English pointer and setter.

Terrain

This is the bird to hunt if you like steep hills, drop-off cliffs, dust-creek bottoms interlaced with limbs, the edges of irrigated fields, high chaparral, and brushpiles—in other words, this is your typical tangle-up, sweat-up, walk-up bird. No way of getting him sittin' on your car hood. If you were going to wait and ambush him, the way you can a greater pinnated grouse, I don't know where the ambush could take place.

The California quail is leg-aching work to find, but the most gratifying to encounter. Surely, it is one of the most delicious to bring to the table.

Talk about serious. This English pointer came to work at dawn, intends to work until dark, and when he points you'd better get a move on, and when you shoot—don't miss. Check those eyes!

8

Mountain Quail

*Navy SEALs, Airborne, Marines, and Rangers should be
trained on mountain quail. They are an impossible objective that live in tortuous terrain. Should a hunter get three
birds a day, he's had a bonanza.*

ONLY A MASOCHIST would hunt mountain quail. They come to bag as a
coincidental treasure when hunting other arid or semi-arid birds. The
temperature is hot when the season opens on mountain quail, their
habitat is vertical, and the vegetation (at least in California) is manzanita: so matted and dense the hunter must crawl on all fours to get
from one clearing to the next. All the while, mind you, you're crawling
in Elsinore diamondback rattlesnake country.

Mountain Treasure

Bill Parton, who accompanied our Gambel's hunt, tells us, "Mountain
quail were like finding gold to me." Bill lived in California during his
youth. "They are our biggest—and most beautiful—quail, what with
their steel-blue hue and the two long plumes coming out. When I was
a kid working in a taxidermy shop, I'd hear successful hunters say they
whistled for them. What they'd do is walk or drive the higher ridges
and whistle down until they got a response. Then they'd take their dog

at heel—and it's mostly crawling as opposed to walking—and work their way down, getting close enough to provoke a flush.

Hunting Tactics

"In doing this, the dog and I have gotten close enough for two or three shots. And, in all my life, I've only been able to get a single bird up two or three times. That's a rare event.

"I have gotten into mountain quail at other places where the brush wasn't so dense. But the terrain is always vertical."

Parton expands on this by saying, "I was working on an Oregon ranch as a hunting guide and I found mountain quail in fairly open country along with chukar. There was a lot of rimrock chukar ground, and the birds were on the edge of that."

Something Special

"There's kind of a haunting effect with mountain quail," says Parton.

Possibly the most unique gamebird of them all and certainly the most elusive: the mountain quail. His plume outdoes any drum major's, and he's got enough distinctive markings to make him a collector's dream. (Photo by Ron Spomer)

"It's like finding a herd of javelina. They're sort of sublime and trusting. They're not real antsy or jumpy.

"It's not a great tactical battle like it is with Gambel's. There you think the bird is running, and you're doing a lot of responding. With mountain quail, you just kind of go to them, whistling and hoping for a response, being real stealthy, and hoping you get close enough for a shot."

Carry a Light Gun

Since this is a quick-jumping bird, often getting up 40 yards or so ahead of you, a full-choked shotgun seems a necessity. It delivers a tight pattern a long distance. Yes, you've got to be an excellent shot.

A light 20-gauge over-and-under or side-by-side is the ticket. We'll forgo the heavier-firing 12-gauge because of the taxing terrain. Who wants to carry that extra weight all day, when the country's straight up and down, and the temperature may be 100 degrees?

No. 6 shot is preferred for distant covey rises in mountainous country. Switch to 7½s if you just can't connect. Should you be able to find mountain quail in relatively flat country, then 7½s would be preferred because you might be shooting over a rare point.

Characteristics

Mountain quail loft high on takeoff and provide a good shot, but they are also adept at putting any obstacle that exists between the gun and themselves.

They'll usually be encountered on heavily shrubbed slopes or in stream bottoms choked with brush. These birds purposely select a heavy overstory for roosting, nesting, and loafing. Their favorite cover is within or below piñon trees.

Mountain quail can be described as a true wilderness gamebird; they avoid housing subdivisions and dense farming. They want nothing to do with man. You'll find them among juniper, willow, wild rose, cottonwood, mountain sage, bush grass, antelope sage, and rabbit brush. In the summer, they feed on seeds, pine nuts, acorns, and fruits. Winter fare is green leafage and buds. They typically roost off the ground in the center of a piñon tree or any shrub that's over 5 feet tall.

Mountain quail are our largest quail, weighing 18 ounces on the average (bobwhites run from 6 to 8 ounces). Mountain quail are also

1 foot long. They make quite a prize to bring to hand because they are so rare, so wily, and large. The mountain and Mearns are the two quail I want mounted and displayed on my fireplace mantel.

Mountain quail are distinguished by a chestnut throat and belly, gray breast, barred flanks, and two long, straight feathers that rise from the center of the head. On the wing, the gunner cannot miss the black-and-white stripes on the chestnut sides. If close enough, he would have to see the two-feathered plume that rises nearly half the length of a standing bird.

California quail occupy the same territory as the mountain quail, but they are easily distinguished from each other because the crest of the California quail is shorter; it also curves out over the bird's eyes in a definite tear drop. Also, the California quail has dull brown flanks with streaks of white. Both male and female mountain quail are similar in appearance.

When hunting desert quail, let your gun dog run to any water hole he can find, both to drink and to soak his belly. Remember, a dog's underbelly is comparable to a human's wrists: that's where the largest supply of superficial blood vessels lie closest to the surface of the skin. This is where you should concentrate your coolant for a heated dog.

The birds are found in eastern Washington, Oregon, California, and northern Baja, with a meager population in Idaho and Nevada. Like a professional golfer, these birds follow warm weather, migrating upward in spring and coming down to valley floors in the winter.

The birds are dependent on water, especially their young, so do not bypass any seepage, spring, irrigation ditch, or pond. For the most likely encounters, check all water sources before 10 o'clock in the morning.

You Need a Unique Gun Dog

Seldom can a dog point mountain quail. The birds are gone the moment they detect you. So the real value of a dog is to follow you at heel and find deadfall once you've been lucky enough to knock it down. Consequently, a retriever or any pointer trained to fetch is a perfect mountain quail dog.

I hunt mountain quail exclusively with Labrador retrievers because finding the bird after its been shot is more important to me than finding them in the first place. I cannot drop a bird and leave without bringing it to bag. As revealed elsewhere in this book, the popular desert dog seems to be the German wirehaired pointer, who will do an excellent job. The wirehaired pointing griffon and the pudelpointer also are good choices. With the harsh brush, a dog with short, close-fitting hair would be at a disadvantage.

The only requirement for any mountain quail dog is that he heel and cast only when ordered to do so. A hunting retriever can be cast to lift the birds, but you'd better be ready for a long shot.

Another Taste Treat

I bring this bird to table flavored with chopped onions, sliced black olives, and large mild green peppers, halved. Sauté these ingredients in a frying pan with 2 tbls. olive oil, then pour over quail breasts that have been grilled over charcoal. (Be sure to crack the breastbone so the meat will lie flat.) A blending accompaniment is potato salad with cold spiced canned green beans.

9

Chukar

"Hunting chukars is a lot like hunting elk. It's a very physical thing. Some people say most of their chukar hunting is on level ground. But in my opinion chukar are kind of an uppity bird: they prefer looking down on everything else. So I find them close to rimrock, next to cliffs, and on top rocky outcroppings."—Mike Gould, of Carbondale, Colorado, expert gun dog trainer, shooting instructor, preserve operator, and hunting guide.

CHUKARS LOVE THE barrens. The great expanses of lonely nothing. Treeless venues with sparse grass, maybe some skiffs of local fescues, bluestem, and predominately cheat grass. Cheat grass starts out bright and lime green in the spring, grows 12 inches tall, and then dies. That's the idea of cheat grass: it tricks us with a spring promise and ends up cheating on us.

The land is disintegrated lava—gritty and abrasive. It can shear a dog's pads off in one day. So outfit Pup with boots. When the season opens in this harsh land, the daytime temperature still hits 100 degrees. So chukar hunting is an endurance contest.

Cutting the Wind

When this bird lofts, it mimics the partridge-type flight that we see with grouse and Hungarians. They actually break into the wind, and

This long-beaked chukar takes the morning sun on a stone. Chukar are where you find them. Las Vegas is America's fastest-growing city, with 4,000 move-ins per month; yet 10 miles from the city limits there are chukars shoulder to shoulder. (Photo by Leonard Lee Rue III)

then fly in a curving pattern downhill. That's their preference: to run uphill and fly downhill. They can outrun a dog.

You can encounter them in really large coveys. Each time they flush, a couple of birds usually stay behind. These are the call-back birds. They sit like glue, and are really good for pointing dogs. So always scour the area of the covey bust.

How to Hunt

One way to hunt chukars is to gain and maintain elevation, working benches or knobs and clumps of vegetation. Always walk into the wind and try to work down—following their call. They won't hold for you if you climb up to them. The birds are very fast in flight, and when shot dead are extremely hard for a dog to find because of their natural camouflage.

Well Armed

Because of the heat and rough terrain, carry the lightest gun you can shoot effectively. Mike Gould recommends a 20- or 28-gauge, side-by-side or over-and-under with 7½ shells. If there is a high wind, switch to 6s. Gould cautions us about using a semiauto, saying, "Almost every time you hear a chukar hunter shoot his third shell, he's unsuccessful. The birds are gone."

Mike also instructs us in shooting, saying, "Ninety-nine percent of all misses are 6 inches above and 18 inches behind. That's because the man quits swinging the gun and lifts his head to peek up. So remember, push the gun through as you fire and keep your head down. That'll get your bird.

"And, each bird has a way of making you miss. For example, the gunner is mesmerized by the twittering pheasant's tail. Consequently, he shoots behind the bird. Most gunners shoot at the breast of a goose, which is the most fortified part of its body. If you can hit a quail, you can hit a goose's head: shoot for the white patch under the jaw. And, the flight characteristics of chukars lead you to believe they are going to continually climb when they come up. They're not. Just as you fire, they break off and dive downhill. So you must arc down slightly on partridge-type birds. Their flight is just part of their survival kit."

The Hunting Retriever

Mike's favorite way of hunting chukars is to position himself downhill, then cast a hunting Labrador retriever upgrade to find and loft the birds—which naturally will fly to the bottom in order to switch back on foot and rapidly climb the hill. With this sandwich method, the gunner is waiting for the bird to fly right to him.

His second preferred hunting method is to monitor the watering holes. In the summer, the chukars go to water several times a day: each time flying down and walking back up. A storied hunt is to take a boat along the Snake River in Idaho and beach when you hear the chukars call. You work your dog toward the call, take your bird, get back in your boat, and float on. Sounds great, doesn't it?

In chukar country, you never try to hunt it all. Just hunt the knolls, benches, and little patches of cover. When objective-hunting, like this, your pointers come into their own. You can cast them into the wind for the likely roosting, feeding, or loafing spots and have a greater chance of success. In this regard, you should remember that the German wirehaired pointer is a favorite for desert bird hunting—for several reasons, but maybe above all because his coat seems best for plants that stick and tear.

Point of Origin

Remember, always carry water for your dog. The chukar lives in arid and semi-arid country. That's understandable; many people say this bird was imported to us from Pakistan, India, and Turkey, though some game biologists say that the successful transplant of chukars occurred in 1935 in the uplands of northern Nevada with Himalayan birds from Nepal.

You'll find chukars in British Columbia, southern Alberta, and Baja, Nevada, Idaho, Utah, western Colorado, Montana, and eastern sections of Washington, Oregon, and California. Scatterings of birds can be found in Arizona, New Mexico, and western South Dakota.

And, oh yes; this is one of the Big 3 of gamebirds that do excellently in captivity: pheasants, bobwhites, and chukars. Preserve chukars are hunted in heavy cover like quail or pheasant.

The Chukar

There is no discernible difference between chukar sexes when the

This hunter drops to one knee to accept the chukar handed up by his Brittany.

birds are on the wing. The gunner sees a gray-blue bird with a black-and-white head pattern, the black-and-chestnut barred flanks, the red legs, and chestnut outer tail feathers. In hand, the male has a stubbed spur.

The best way to tell a chukar is to hear him "chuck." Or, as is often the case, catch their rally call, which comes to our ear as *chuck, chuck-ara,* or *per-chuck*. The call reassembles broken coveys. Remember Bill Parton, the hunting guide, sculptor, and carver of Oracle, Arizona? Regarding these calls, he laughs and says, "Any chukar hunt always ends up with the birds high on a rimrock above you, cackling."

Chukars are excellent fowl for the table, being halfway in size between a bobwhite and a ruffed grouse. Plus, they eat predominately vegetable matter. Their average size is 1½ pounds and they run 12 inches in length.

This Beats a Cardboard Hamburger

Bill Parton has the best way of preparing cooked chukar so far as I'm concerned. He puts several chukar breasts in a crock pot and cooks until done. Then he bones and shreds the meat and puts it back in the broth with a mixture of mild chilies and chunked onions. I add garlic. This is simmered until the flavor is intermixed. Then, he spoons and pours this meat and broth over steamed rice, crispy tortillas, or pasta. With this recipe, whatever grows in the garden can be thrown in the pot with superb results. I call cooking like this a bachelor's delight . . . and for a wife who's got to feed a pack of human-male wolverines, it's a godsend!

Should you ever want to get fancy, however, try this: assemble three whole chukars, a handful of thinly sliced green onions, ¼ cup butter, ½ cup brandy, 2 cups chicken broth, 9 slices bacon, 2 cups heavy cream, ¼ cup freshly grated horseradish, and white pepper to taste.

Melt the butter in a roasting pan. Add onions and cook until transparent – set aside. Add the chukar and cook until well-browned on all sides. Preheat the oven to 375 degrees. When the birds are browned, add brandy – careful of the flame. When flames die, add broth, pepper, and onions. Put 3 slices of bacon on each breast. Roast, uncovered, 35 minutes, basting often. Stir cream and horseradish into au juice. Roast 15 minutes longer.

Eat as is for a feast, or chill and chunk off for great sandwiches.

10

Sage Hen

The sage grouse lives almost exclusively on sage grass and keeps company with lonely winds, vistas of treeless nothing, placid antelope, and wild mustangs. Man comes infrequently to hunt the antelope and capture the horses, but for the most part the sage grouse is left alone.

WHEN I RAN with Dan Opie, he was a frayed-cuff, patched-jean, tattered-straw-hat rancher grubbing to make ends meet on the dust-claimed barrens of eastern Oregon. Then he foaled a quarter horse that became the national halter champion, Sir Quincy Dan, and sold him for $500,000. For the rest of his life, Opie showed up frayed-cuff, patched-jean, and hatted with tattered straw.

He assigned me drag on a cattle drive to move some grade stuff up to BLM summer meadow. A point rider spooked a sage grouse; he rose like a hawk and flapped to a tree-clad stream. Dan Opie dropped back and said to me, "See that sage hen?" I nodded yes. He said, "As a kid in this country roping wild horses for the army and riding them bareback up to 16 miles to a corral, and getting $2 a piece for the doing of it, I shot one of those birds and cooked him in a pot for a week—I still couldn't eat him."

I swore right then I'd never shoot and eat a sage hen. But a man must be careful of what he swears by, for since then the sage grouse has become a favorite of mine both in the field and in the kitchen.

A sage grouse cock displays to attract a mate. (Photo by Leonard Lee Rue III)

The Bomber Bird

This is a giant bird we're talking about: some 22 inches in length, with an average weight of 6½ pounds (but recorded up to 8 pounds). He is also a magnificently beautiful creature, being a white-spotted dark gray-brown on the back with a lower belly patch of black, and a long, pointed tail that is breathtaking drama on the strutting grounds. Why is the tail so startling? Because, unlike on other grouse, the tail feathers are erected separately like rays of the sun or the spiked crown on the Statue of Liberty. Females are smaller and more homogenous in their markings.

Sage grouse are unique in that they do not have a muscular gizzard. Consequently, their thin-walled stomachs require soft foods, which are essentially the leaves of sagebrush, supplemented in summer by leaves and fruits of various plants, as well as the opportune insect that happens by. In winter, sage grouse live almost exclusively on sage grass (being an evergreen, it stays succulent year-round).

Since sage grass is this grouse's food source, cover source, and contentment source, these birds are not found where sage grass does not grow — nor where it is covered with snow in the winter. That's why they top out at about 8,000 feet in the Rockies. By necessity, sage grouse are an arid to semi-arid bird. (Note: sage hens and antelope cannot break the crust of snow to graze; this is done for them by the wild horses. When the horses are gone, the hen and antelope will suffer.)

Behavior

When the snow is minimized, the adult males gather at a lek, that traditional, annual gathering place where males strut and display — primarily with threat stances — that nevertheless have the corollary role of attracting hens for mating. These displays constitute territorial defense with a predominance of ritual fighting and the resultant attraction of a mate. It's all based on hostile threats. To avoid being attacked, females assume submissive postures, and their role is confined to being seen and not heard. Breeding occurs at the lek.

Flight

When lofted, sage grouse display a clumsy takeoff. But don't let that fool you. The bird is actually flying faster than a quail, and he gains momentum as he turns, beating and gliding down off a slope. Sage grouse can also take a heavy load, and once down they are extremely difficult to find because their coloration so closely matches their environment.

The Dog of Choice

You can get stylish points on this big bird with any pointing dog, but it takes the average dog a few days' hunting time before he can adapt to this bird. There are several reasons for this but none more pivotal than the fact that you'll be hunting miles and miles of barrens with no edges, and you'll be putting the dog on a bird with a very distinct odor.

Favored gun dog for this bomber bird is any pointer, be it one of the versatile hunting breeds, an English setter, or a pointer. Of the versatiles, you can't go wrong with a Brittany. The Brittany is a scamper (like the English springer spaniel), and it's a delight to work him in high country where he can run cool and you can see this pocket-size gun dog lift these mighty birds.

However, I've had my best success in the mountains of Colorado with hunting Labs while seeking blue grouse. Where I come upon a single sage hen, I cast the Lab, he lifts the bird, I bring it down, and the dog fetches it.

If you grow tired of walking, then try to locate a waterhole and idle about. You'll see sage grouse tracks and you'll know the birds are frequenting the place. You also can assume two things: first, they'll be back several times that day; and second, during the meantime they'll be close by feeding or loafing. So hunt in ever-broadening circles. Here the Lab has the patience borne of duck hunting to wait hours for the incoming sage grouse.

You'll sometimes find large coveys of sage grouse, but it has been my experience to encounter singles. Understanding their swiftness, I handle them as carefully as bobwhites.

No, folks, this English pointer ain't yawning. He's come up with a long-stretch point to indicate a sage hen. What a first baseman he'd make.

Sage grouse are hard to hunt because at low elevations you're out there in arid and semi-arid lands with soaring temperatures and no shade. As with other desert birds, carry water for yourself and your dog. A wet year makes it easier going for the hunter, but at the same time makes the birds harder to find.

Since a sage grouse's terrain is vast, you need to flat out cast your pointers to fly and cover as much ground as possible—because you know the dog has been trained to whoa, pinning the bird to immobility, until you get there.

Since you're going to get points on sage grouse, you need only carry a 20-gauge over-and-under or side-by-side shotgun. Shoot low-brass 6s; you're trying to knock down a bird that can have twice the weight of a pheasant.

Distribution

You can find sage grouse in Washington, Oregon, northeastern California, Idaho, almost all of Nevada, southern Idaho, northwestern and central Utah, a bit of Canada above Montana, all of Montana, most all of Wyoming, some of Colorado, and small patches of North and South Dakota, with a trace in Nebraska and small patches in northern New Mexico. This bird has a vast distribution, but check each state's fish and game department: there are places where there are no open seasons on sage grouse, or in some cases, very limited seasons and restricted possession limits.

Sage grouse were once threatened by habitat depletion because ranchers and farmers were converting sage-grass range to irrigated farming. Not only have millions of acres of sage grass been removed during this century, but the introduction of herbicides has also wreaked havoc.

The annual up-and-down migration of sage grouse is opposite that of blue grouse. In winter, the sage grouse come down, the blue grouse go up. The strutting grounds are at the lower elevations. No matter the direction, adult males are the last to migrate.

Bringing the Bomber to Table

Well, the big question becomes how to prepare a sage grouse for the table. First off, the preparation is not as important as the cleaning. Sage grouse must be cleaned fast. Never forget this, and get your carcass chilled as quickly as possible.

Long ago, I began cooking sage grouse the same way I cook geese.

Make a basket of aluminum foil, place the cleaned bird in the center, pour in 1 liter of Coke, fold and crimp the foil air tight, then bake in a pan until done (determined by a poultry thermometer that registers 185 degrees when placed in the breast). Caution: split and spread back the aluminum so it doesn't touch the thermometer.

But should you have company, this recipe is my favorite. Grind 1 raw breast (you need 2 cups) and combine with 1½ tsp. salt, 1 tsp. black pepper, 4 cloves garlic, 1 tbls. Tabasco, ½ cup bread crumbs, 1 egg, and sufficient whole cream to form into patties about 3 inches in diameter and ½-inch-thick.

Dip patties on both sides in melted butter and flour and dip again. Broil to brown on both sides, and brush with melted butter as patties cook. Serve with hot oil and spinach salad with a side of tomatoes and okra.

Also, don't forget the tail feathers. I like to include them in personal letters to favored friends. They drop out to make a happy surprise.

11

Blue Grouse

While hunting and fishing around the world, I've never met a man or woman who knew more about a particular game species than Mike Gould knows about blue grouse. Mike, you'll recall, is the gun dog trainer, hunting guide, and game preserve operator in Carbondale, Colorado.

THE LETTER'S DATED Aug. 23, 1989. It's written on blue-lined yellow notebook paper. The writing is lumpy, unevenly spaced. The *c*'s look like *i*'s, the *u*'s look like *n*'s. Mike writes, "I left for the high country about 4:30 this morning. I headed for the flat tops so I could be there by first light. I had 2 English pointers, 2 English setters, 2 German shorthairs, 2 Labs, and, of course, Web."

Web is the best assistant training pro I ever met. He is a black Lab who wrote the book on hunting retrievers.

Mike continues, "I saw 50 blue grouse by 9:00, and every single one of those young dogs were on birds. All of the pointing dogs got to point at least once and several got backing practice.

"I was running Web as a strike dog for those young pointers. When Web would find a covey, I would blow him down as the first bird left, then he would sit and watch as we worked the young pointers in.

"Once a little orange-and-white pointer had pointed his first covey, he stood there while the 2 shorthairs and one of the setters crowded in front of him and pointed. There it was, four young dogs, all pointing the covey, and Web sitting off to side. We got up 7 birds.

Blue grouse hens nest amidst the protective cover of conifers and mast. (Photo by Charles G. Summers, Jr., of Leonard Rue Enterprises)

"I noticed a harrier working the ridge above me. I knew then the grouse were in the park, and I would find them. Seeing a harrier tells you he's above blue grouse. I really don't think harriers hit the grouse, they have very small feet, and mainly feed on smaller prey. The blues ignore them, but let a goshawk come over and they go dead, squatting flat to the ground.

"I call the harrier, 'Grouse omen,' for they are almost constantly over the shoulder of a grouse hunter, if there are any grouse around.

"When our training session was over, I reviewed the past 15 days: I saw a total of over 500 antelope, 93 bucks, 67 does, 427 blue grouse, 24 sage grouse, 8 bull elk, 9 cows, and I saw three coyotes twice. I saw two badgers in the same day, 10 miles apart. I saw one fox and many raptors and lots of small game.

"I saw a half-dozen young dogs find themselves, forever. I never even spoke harsh to one of them. They learned the most beautiful lesson, 'How to find birds.' I was knee-deep in covey after covey of blue grouse and could have picked virtually any direction to work. I was at 10,100 feet at daylight and back at the ranch by lunch, day after day.

"My wish for you, Bill, is that a harrier is always working the ridge above you, for then you will know the grouse are in the park, and you will find them."

The serious gun dog trainer would do well to hole up in Carbondale, Colorado, during the latter part of August and the first part of September any year and train at 10,000 feet on blue grouse. The birds hold interminably for a young dog. When they loft, they explode as one covey. You can follow the busted covey and work the dog on singles, though it's not absolutely necessary because there are so many coveys to work.

The Blue Grouse

There are eight subspecies of blue grouse, but the one we hunt resides in the Colorado mountains and is called the dusky blue grouse or *Dendragapus obscurus*. These birds reside in the Rockies from central Wyoming and western South Dakota south through eastern Utah and Colorado to northeastern Arizona and northwestern New Mexico. The range of all eight subspecies stretches across British Columbia into Yukon Territory.

What the Birds Eat

Now, there's a particular venue in which to seek these beautiful birds. They love to congregate in male aspen stands. Let me explain. The best time to sex an aspen tree is in late June or July when the buds appear. The male buds are much larger than the female aspen buds. The male buds are also much richer in protein, fat, and minerals. The blue grouse do not seem to eat the female buds, or at least, they don't prefer them.

Aspens grow in clumps called clones. All of the trees in a specific clone are of the same sex.

Other vegetation favored by blue grouse include fescue grass, chokecherries, willows, and serviceberry. They ply the quakie pockets, rimrocks, tops of ridges, and seeping springs. Their favorite escape maneuver is to loft and then suddenly curve down. That's why they are so easily missed by gunners: it's intuitively hard to pull your barrel down when swinging through.

Blue grouse are trusting at the first part of the season, but they get mighty flighty as gunning nears.

Mike Gould says, "It's up to the hunter to read the land and the bird and get the good shooting opportunities." Consequently, when I've been blue grouse hunting with him, he has not kept his dogs in close.

Rather, he runs them uphill as much as he can and lets 'em hit a lick. In tight country, he calls them in a little bit. But if it's open with big mountain meadows he just, as he says, "Cranks 'em up and lets them fly."

Preferred shot for blue grouse are 7½s with 6s a close second. Shoot a lightweight 20- or 28-gauge over-and-under or side-by-side. Remember, you're at 8,000 to 10,000 feet, and if you're not in shape, you're going to be mighty winded, light-headed, and leg-tired.

The Sunshine Bird

Also remember, you might be there on a great, sunshiny day, and the blue grouse live in this habitat at this altitude, and they must daily seek the sun for survival. That's why they gravitate toward ridges and rims. They are very sensitive to good exposure, for not only does the sun shine warm on them there, but it also sustains their food sources.

Wind-blown ridges and rims will provide lots of berries, bush grass, and even legume mixes near a water seep. Willows near the water and a stand of aspens nearby complete the ideal grouse habitat.

This feisty English setter and I bag another Rocky Mountain blue grouse. (Photo by Bill Berlat)

Yes, blue grouse are also found in coniferous forests, but not in the numbers they are encountered in the great mountain parks. And they essentially seek these dense, old-stand forests with lots of downfall in the winter. Such an environment supports thimbleberry and currants, which, along with the Douglas fir and Englemann spruce needles, will sustain the blues.

Typically, blue grouse occupy the foothills in the spring, moving up to timberline by winter. Gould and I usually conduct our blue grouse hunts at 8,000 feet where, coincidentally, we also encounter sage hens. Some biologists contend that blues and sages are related: they point specifically to the similarity of their respective chicks in the down.

Characteristics

Blue grouse are large gamebirds; males measure 21 inches and weigh an average of 4 pounds. A standing male looks slick – like a duck – and in flight is noted for his dark gray color, the 1- inch light blue bar at the terminus of his tail, and the white flash found on his cheek, throat, and under-tail coverts. If close at hand, you can see the yellow dash of bare skin over each eye as well as the bare neck patches – ranging from yellow to lavender – which are exposed when posing for a prospective mate.

The female is a pale, mottled brown – resembling the color of a female pheasant – and though she has similar areas of bare skin, they are much smaller and less pronounced.

Through Mike Gould's letter we learn that any gun dog will serve well on blue grouse. Hunt them as you would the bobwhite. Cast for objectives, hunt the edges, seek the ideal food sources, and always cast into the wind.

Preparing for Table

When the hunt is over, clean these great birds and save them for a summer meal by storing them in waxed 2-quart milk cartons filled with water. The frozen water preserves the meat: no freezer burn.

To make a marinade, pulverize a clove of garlic and combine with 2 tbls. olive oil, four dashes of lime juice, and three dashes of black pepper in a nonmetal baking dish.

Cut the grouse in short strips and coat both sides in marinade. Poultry slices better when partially frozen. Let stand 1 hour.

Place two minced garlic cloves and 1 chopped onion in 2 tbls. olive oil and sauté until onions appear transparent. Stir two sliced garden-fresh tomatoes, two small sliced bell peppers, a dash of coriander, and 1 tbls. of chili powder into the onion mixture. Splash with 2 tsp. of lime juice.

Prepare charcoal for the fire. Remove grouse strips from the marinade, and grill to taste over white coals. Spatula onto a soft tortilla, cover with marinade (which is our salsa), and mate with fresh summer corn accompanied with the heads of green onions—all rolled up in aluminum foil and covered with butter. The corn and onions are placed on the grill at least 10 minutes before the grouse strips. Serve with lots of iced tea.

Ole! You now have a blue grouse fajita. Enjoy.

12

Ruffed Grouse and Woodcock

Have you ever pulled the cord on a Venetian blind—the old wooden-slat kind—and it got away from you to cascade down and clatter on the windowsill making a sound so startling it almost lifted you out of your shoes? Well, that's the effect of a ruffed grouse—secreted in cover—who lingers until the last possible moment only to explode 1 yard before your feet. He seemingly launches straight up— only at the same time, the bird is twisting and hurtling through branches that defy passage. You shoot, and branches snap loose and bark curls away and leaves fall shredded, but the ruffed grouse beats on.

HE'S THE OUTDOOR treasure of New England, like the Nene goose (a protected bird that lives high on Haleakala Mountain) is to Hawaii, the Mearns is to the Sonoran desert, the pheasant is to mid-America, and the bobwhite is to Dixie. That doesn't mean you won't find the ruffed grouse all across the North American and Canadian woodlands, even dipping down into Northern California, but it's New England that has raised him to mystique status.

There's no reason he shouldn't earn our admiration. He's hard to find, hard to work with a dog, hard to flush, and hard to shoot on the wing. An avid grouse hunter will wear out a good pair of hunting boots a season chasing this guy. The brush tangles where Mr. Ruffed Grouse lives defy a breezy walk-through.

Mearns quail hunter Jim Pettijohn of Sedona, Arizona, won best of show in the amateur division at the World Decorative Bird Carving Tournament with this ruffed grouse. (Photo by Jim Pettijohn)

Dog Work

I cast my Brittany, Brandy, into the thicket before me, urging him to plow into the briar patches, weed barriers, logpiles, and the high grass grown in abandoned apple orchards. Brandy also knows what an aspen stand is (I showed him), and he's always to check there, plus any spruce trees he comes across—for grouse like to lazy up there, especially in a snow storm. To find them feeding in winter, Brandy checks all stands of aspen, willows, catkins, hazelnut, wild cherry, and apple, where the birds perch and eat buds, fruit, leaves, and twigs.

Brandy's also learned to sniff all snowbanks, for grouse have the remarkable trait of diving headlong into them; they'll bury themselves, and their body heat helps them survive a cold winter's night. A few grouse have been lost when iced rain or deep snow came and sealed the entry hole shut, but more have fallen prey to a fox who also knew to look for holes in the snow.

The Drummer with Snowshoes

Known as the "little drummer" for rearing back on his fantail and beating the air with cupped wings during mating season, the ruffed grouse has the unique capability of growing "snowshoes" in the winter. Actually, biologists say the ruffed grouse sprouts scalelike pectinations on his feet. These help him grasp ice-coated branches and walk on soft snow. The bird maintains two definite color phases and two habitats. In his southern range, he is red; up north and west, he is gray. There's a ruff around his (and her) neck from whence he gets his name. His head is crowned with a crest, and he sports a narrow slash of featherless skin over the eyes, which is orange in most males, a blue-gray for the distaff. He needs evergreens to survive the winter, but summers amidst hardwood and brush with lots of clearings for dusting and sunning. He measures some 16 to 19 inches long, weighs 1 1/2 pounds, and can fly over 20 m.p.h.

His supporters say no finer bird can be brought to the table, and he is usually prepared with sauces, wines, and spices. To be invited to a New England grouse feast means someone owes you something.

The Gun to Use

This bird can be taken with either a 20- or 28-gauge shotgun shooting 7 1/2s or 8s. Improved cylinder would do nicely, but if the bird keeps getting away from you, then go to a modified choke. As for me, I carry a thirty-year-old 20-gauge Beretta Golden Snipe with 26-inch barrels, bored improved and modified.

How to Hunt

Now—how do we hunt this elusive bird with a dog?

Easy. From early training on, the dog must stop immediately upon the detection of a scent cone. He must whoa, which means he puts all four feet flat and doesn't move an eyelid.

If the dog will point this far distant, and you are an accurate enough shot, you'll get grouse. For the dog stays put, you analyze what's before him, learn to know likely habitat, and go there, shuffling about, ever with the gun poised and your heart ready for an explosion at your feet.

An extra bonus of ruffed grouse hunting is the beautiful country. Here grouse guide George Hickox stops to love his Llewellyns in wonderful Nova Scotia: cascading streams, no litter, few hunters, fewer native gun dogs, and miles of no inhabitants.

If the dog crowds the scent cone, you will never get a bird unless one hits a tree trunk, bounces off dazed, and you step on it. All your grouse training must be to this one end: making the dog super-sensitive to the scent cone where he stops at the minimum stimulus. Then he must not catwalk, not barge in, not relocate. He must stand there and let you do the hunting with gun at port arms.

The second imperative of a grouse dog is he must hunt close to the gunner. Any pointing dog can be trained to examine every nearby hideaway. Matter of fact, an English pointer was the 1993 national grouse and woodcock champion. In that regard, any of Bob Wehle's English pointers will work grouse, if you know how to train them and get a handle on them early and never relinquish it. I mention Bob, for he is the world's foremost gun dog breeder – all breeds. However, the English setter is the storied companion for these woods and this bird. The Elhew pointer strain will be mentioned again below.

Since grouse dogs work in such heavy cover, it benefits both dog and hunter if the dog wears either a bell on his leather collar or a beeper collar. Both devices will tell you where the dog is, plus the beeper collar will tell you if the dog is still hunting or is stationary on point.

Any dog can fetch; that's not a factor here. The dog will get your downed bird. But to get you the shot – that's the dog's ultimate responsibility. He must be trained. No junkyard dog is going to point you a ruffed grouse.

The Woodcock

Finally, we must discuss the woodcock, the timberdoodler, so named because of his trait of flying through tree trunks. You swear that's the only way he could have gotten away – by zigzagging through timber that, seemingly, a .22 bullet couldn't penetrate.

Yes, the woodcock is the mud-bird, who lives on worms, stinks something horrible to a gun dog, and has driven many a would-be hunter to throw his gun in a creek.

That men want to hunt this bird proves that some seek a certain amount of self-flagellation. The woodcock is hard to find, a mess to hunt (what with his penchant for timber-clad streams and soft mud banks), is generally despised by dogs – most won't fetch him up – and is nearly impossible to hit with No. 8 shot. But the woodcock has created zealots who prefer him above all other gamebirds. Matter of fact, a duo woodcock hunt and Atlantic salmon fishing outing is considered the ultimate of sport by many.

Here's a male woodcock "peenting" (his call is a nasal peent) on singing ground. This nocturnal bird will let a dog work close and then explode to flight. (Photo by Leonard Lee Rue III)

Conformation

In flight, a woodcock looks like a fat badminton shuttlecock with a 16D finish nail for a nose and eyes in the back of his head. That's right, with his snoot always in the ground probing for worms, his face is flat to the mud, so his eyes are set far back so he can see any predator that might come upon him. He is mottled Van Dyke brown in color, so closely resembling the forest floor where he lives that he can crouch there, right before your eyes, and be impossible to detect. All in all, he is as logically and symmetrically constructed as a moose. Both were created by some committee from spare parts.

Another Kind of Shorebird

A migratory shorebird who essentially left his calling, the woodcock is larger than a bobwhite, some 11 inches long, weighing 6 ounces, and can hit 30 m.p.h. before a gun. His range in the United States stretches from New England to Kansas, where I've hunted him on many a timber-clad, mud-bank creek.

Hunt this bird with a short-barreled 20-gauge shotgun shooting No. 8s. Be ready; you'll have several double flushes. And show him to the neighbor kids, for it's likely they'll never see another unless they become a woodcock hunter.

The Dog

Your grouse dog will do nicely on woodcock. Any dog that hunts close and does not crowd the scent cone is required. However, this bird will sit tight before a dog, but let the hunter get near and he will explode to flight. The woodcock feeds primarily at night, so you'll usually find him asleep on a day's hunt. Therefore, the dog must concentrate his search in good cover; for the bird sure ain't going to sleep on the open flats. This year's running saw nine setters, eight pointers, and two Brittanies vie for the North American Woodcock Championship. It was won by Boston's Dr. David Calcagni's Elhew Gamemaster, a male pointer just out of his canine "teens." The week before, the same dog won the Northeast Grouse Championship.

But any of the continental breed can work both grouse and woodcock.

Time to Eat

The woodcock is favored at the table and can be brought there with the same recipe and same grill as the bobwhite.

I like them prepared as follows: Force a little salt pork under the skin of the breast before grilling. Season with butter, salt and pepper, lemon juice, and pulverized garlic cloves. Wrap woodcock in bacon and grill for a taste delight.

For ruffed grouse, assemble the following: Two ruffed grouse cut for frying, 4 cloves garlic, 1/3 cup vegetable oil, 6 sliced carrots, 6 small sliced onions, 6 small sliced turnips, 6 medium sliced potatoes, 1 large stalk sliced celery, 6 cups water, 1 tsp. salt, 1/2 tsp. oregano, 2 tbls. medium hot chile, 1 tsp. coriander, 1 cup white wine.

Heat oil in a pot, add garlic, and cook until heated. Add grouse sections, and cook until browned on all sides. Remove from the pot. Add sliced vegetables and stir until browned on edges. Replace grouse pieces atop vegetables. Add water, salt, chile, coriander, and 3/4 cup wine. Bring to boil, reduce heat, cover, and simmer 45 minutes. Serve with remaining 1/4 cup wine.

A Word about Weather

Bad weather can drive gamebirds to cover and wipe out any hunt. But nowhere is this more applicable than ruffed grouse. Here's why.

First, a late fall means the apples have not dropped from the abandoned apple trees, and there's no reason to coax the grouse out into open venues. Ruffed grouse don't want to eat hard apples; they want them mushy and fermented.

Why should this make any difference? Well, grouse cover is so intertangled and impenetrable the hunter should carry a chain saw. So, many hunters wait for the grouse to come to the tote roads for gravel and/or enter the apple orchards where there's clear shooting.

Second, rain can wipe out most any bird hunt, but it's especially tough on ruffed grouse. You can't get through grouse cover when it's dry, and when it's wet you are in absolute misery. Plus the birds have hunkered down; they are impossible to find.

Consequently, the worse grouse hunting is when the year's stayed too hot for too long, and you must go meet this guy in a downpour.

With woodcock, it's just the opposite on heat: an early freeze will drive him south, a warm fall will keep him longer in the field for you to find.

13

Doves and Pigeons

It is estimated that 20 million mourning doves (so named for their mournful call) are killed annually. This is more than all waterfowl combined. They are the sportiest of all gamebirds, and it is a rare hunter who collects a legal limit of doves with only one box of shells.

AMONG THE DOVES and pigeons found in the United States, only three are recognized as gamebirds: the mourning dove, the whitewing dove, and the bandtail pigeon. Only the first two concern us, and the whitewing is really a bird hunted more in Mexico than the United States. (Matter of fact, they are slaughtered there, and we seem helpless in stopping it.)

Doves and pigeons are relatively streamlined birds with heads that appear too small for their bodies. The mourning dove is gray with a pen tail, the whitewing dove is gray with a white wing patch, and the bandtail pigeon has a broad gray tip on its fanned tail, plus a yellow bill and white neck band.

A mourning dove is about 12 inches long, weighs some 5 ounces, and I've clocked him flying beside my car at 60 m.p.h. Everybody knows this bird for his call and his insistence (like the bobwhite quail) in living close to humans. Plus, the mourning dove nests in all forty-eight contiguous states. The whitewing dove and bandtail pigeon are relatively obscure in the United States because they are regional—and the bandtail pigeon has a very limited hunting season, if any season at

Bill Koelpin's carving knife and paintbrush say this is what a mourning dove looks like. Who are we to argue? (Photo by Mark Deprez)

all. Both the whitewing dove and bandtail pigeon are bigger and slower than the mourning dove.

Catch Me If You Can

I know of no other bird that can fly like a mourning dove. He *was* where your shot *went*. He is known not only for breakneck speed and sudden braking, but also for dipping, rising, and generally doing a hula dance while all these other gymnastics are going on. Might as well try to hit a butterfly.

The essential scheme we use to harvest this gamebird is bush-whacking him midst his habitual daily rounds. You see, the bird likes seeds. So you'll naturally find him frequenting a cattle feedlot, and you take your stand there. Sitting on a galvanized 1-gallon bucket in a sesame field will produce more doves than if you were secreted in a corn, peanut, sunflower, or soybean field (though the last four can prove very attractive to this bird). However in a pinch, I think any field with seeds of grass, cultivated crops, or weeds will do.

Doves and pigeons are among the few birds that must have water to drink. So, you waylay them at farm ponds where you've taken a hide under a small tree, or behind a pile of weeds, bushes, or sticks. Expect them in about 4 o'clock in the afternoon.

Your chances of increasing sightings and getting doves into range are enhanced with the placement of a half-dozen decoys, either papier-maché, formed plastic, or carved wood blocks.

Many doves are shot from telephone wires where they like to congregate and sit close to gravel for their gizzards. But it's generally against the law to shoot from a public right-of-way, and such hunters are asking for arrest.

Not every hunter favors this bird at the table, for they have very dark meat. And, it is generally agreed that dogs despise them. But there's a reason for this and it can be avoided, as we'll see later.

Handling Pup in Hot Weather

You must learn to handle a hot dog. Rather, how to handle a cool dog in hot weather. For that's the secret: never let the retriever get hot in the first place.

All the way out of town you keep Pup under cross-ventilation or air-conditioning. If you're traveling dirt roads and don't want dust in the car, then stow Pup in a kennel crate and toss in a block of ice. He'll love it.

When you get to the dove field, walk slowly to your stand and

In high heat and humidity, a dove dog often needs to be cooled off. These thoughtful hunters have toted gallons of water and a big tub to field so Pup can jump into a chilled spa.

Dick Cook of Topping, Virginia, is rapidly becoming the top miniature gamebird carver in America. Here one of his mourning doves rapidly passes a brace of training whistles. (Photo by Dick Cook)

force Pup to say at heel all the way. If you let him tear about the place, he'll be stepping on his tongue by the time you're ready to set up.

Once you've arrived at your stand, give Pup a drink of cold water from his canteen. If you're right-handed, pull Pup's lower-left lip away from his gums, make a trough of the lip, and pour water into the trough. Gauge the flow. Pour no more than Pup can lap.

Watering finished, tell Pup, "Sit . . . stay." Such commands are all part of basic yard-training. Should Pup be afield without such a background, tie him to your stool or put his leash under your foot – do whatever's necessary to keep him from moving about.

Some fifteen minutes after the first watering, water Pup again. Then, in another fifteen minutes, water him again. The secret to all this is keep Pup cool and he can fetch all day, but let him get hot and you'll never cool him down. *Never.* Once heated, he'll start to pant, which will bring slobber, and the slobber will turn to suds, and Pup will not retrieve.

Dogs refuse to fetch doves because the froth of their hot mouths sticks to the feathers and pulls them from the bird. The dog chokes on them and fusses with them in his mouth – trying to spit them out.

Canine saliva is just like glue. Try to pick a glob of it from the kennel floor – it just strings out! Soft dove feathers adhere to the saliva, and Pup fights to get rid of them.

If you keep the dog cool, keep his mouth water-slick, he will fetch all day with no grudge.

When Pup does make a retrieve and delivers to hand, take the bird, lay it aside, then dress Pup's muzzle with both hands, wiping away any grass or feathers that might be stuck.

Throughout the hunt keep giving Pup fresh water. Keep him prone. And keep him in the shade. Plus, should there be a block of ice in the car, lay it on the dirt, move it, and let Pup lay in the wet, cold spot left behind.

Also, never pull a bird from Pup's mouth, always push it. That's right, take the bird in hand, then gently turn it toward his eyes and press it forward. This will naturally open Pup's jaws, and he'll release his hold.

Should Pup, for some reason, refuse to give you the bird (this happens sometimes when a bird is shot up), either blow an abrupt blast of air directly into his nose or reach over, curl the forefinger of your hand about that flap of skin that runs from Pup's back leg to his waist, and literally pick up the dog. He will let loose of the bird.

Gun dog of choice for doves is any dog who will patiently sit, can take the hot sun, and can retrieve.

Rattlesnakes: Another Peril

Another caution for your retriever: dove hunts are hot-weather hunts, so in some regions you can expect rattlesnakes. I was hunting doves

Coming upwind on a rattler, this pointer has stopped with all the abruptness of a cutting horse. Think ahead in dove season and direct your dog from all possible hazards.

The term stool pigeon *originally meant a pigeon decoy that duped other pigeons to net or gun. This nineteenth-century stool pigeon, with a wooden body and metal tail, found its way from England to my bookshelf, where it hasn't lured a pigeon in forty years.*

just south of Phoenix, Arizona, next to irrigated cotton. The farmer stopped and mentioned that that summer he had counted 500 rattlesnakes just across the road from where I was set up. When the water enters the irrigation ditches, the mice go to the mounds, where the snakes await them. I got out of there fast; there is nothing more important to me than my dogs.

The Gun to Use

Doves are shot with any gauge gun (except the .410) and usually with 7½s or 8s. Take enough shells. I've heard that the national average is four shells per dove. This is the bird that will give you a shooting lesson. And remember, this is a migratory bird that comes under the jurisdiction of the federal government. Know your regulations.

I bring this bird to table baked, roasted, or grilled with lots of spices. For best results, discard the backbone and break the breastbone between butt of palm and counter, marinate the dove for at least 12 hours in 1 cup white wine, ½ cup olive oil, 1 tsp. salt, 1 tsp. black pepper, 1 cup tomato puree, 3 pulverized garlic cloves, and 1 tsp. oregano.

Grill over white embers. Serve with lots of fresh green onions, navy beans, and a baked potato.

14

Prairie Chickens

The Flint Hills of east-central Kansas—lush, rolling prai-
rie that stretches from Topeka to the Oklahoma border—
is the bluegrass capital of the world. Herds of cattle graze
there, and ranchers guard the insularity of the region with
zeal. A few years ago, a federal helicopter landed on one
of the ranches, and the dignitaries alighted to tell the
exasperated rancher they wanted to make part of this
vast, empty, wind-blown expanse a prairie park. The
rancher told them to get their damned machine off his
property and never come back. They never have.

The reason I highlight the Flint Hills is that they are
home to the largest population of prairie chickens in the
world, and a place where I left a toenail under every rock.

THERE ARE TWO prairie chickens: the greater and lesser pinnated
grouse. You find the big birds in Kansas, with a possible smattering in
Michigan, Minnesota, North and South Dakota, Nebraska, Colorado,
Oklahoma, and Texas. The lessers are found in the latter two states.

I'll write of both as one bird. The prairie chicken is as big as its
namesake, the domestic chicken. It weighs over 2 pounds, measures
some 18 inches, and I've clocked them at 40 m.p.h. The male has a
courting ritual that has inspired Plains Indians to don feather bustles
and stamp around in circles. That's what the chicken does. Plus, he
erects his neck feathers, fans his tail, blows air sacks located beneath

Two prairie chickens square off on a Bill Koelpin battlefield. (Photo by Mark Deprez)

and to the sides of his head, and fights like hell with any interlopers. All this takes place on "booming" grounds, which the Indians emulate with powwows.

How to Hunt

The Flint Hills are nearly the last great stand of native tall-grass prairie in the United States. The roots go many feet down; break them with a mechanized plow, and they retort like a rifle shot. These grasses were eons in the making. And the flinty gravels of the topsoil here prompted would-be nesters to look farther west in Kansas for suitable farmland.

(Incidentally, the only trees in the Flint Hills are found in the valleys or abrupt breaks in the earth. There they not only can find sufficient moisture to withstand a drought, but are buried enough to escape the many prairie fires.)

Sure, you can take off across this endless prairie and hunt prairie chickens like you would bobwhites. But the prairie chicken is found on tops of rounded knolls, where he is wary as radar. I've walked miles to kick up a covey. The only way I've been able to approach is through the concealment of a slope and a heavy wind.

The bird eats both animal and vegetable matter. But has one penchant: soybeans.

Thus, the best way to hunt prairie chicken is to take a stand along a fencerow before a soybean field. I've done that south of Emporia, Kansas, where you arrive in the dark to set up, and you think you've got it made. But when the sun claims the horizon, you find you're there with a hundred people — all lined up along the fencerow. I hate hunting like this.

Jim Culbertson (I've spoken of him before) is my thirty-year hunting companion who taught me tons about the field and game. Jim and I were crouched down on the fencerow when here they came. The chickens leave their roost and fly in clumps, using the wind, moving steadily, when they drop to glide into the soybean field to feed. The guns bark like Normandy. And Jim connects — he always connects. He shoots this Winchester Model 12 with full choke for every bird. (Regarding quail, he says they quit their acrobatics at 35 yards, so he waits to shoot them from that distance on to 75 yards. Yes, he hits. Never bet him.)

And I'll make this one observation: birds can be shot at 80 yards.

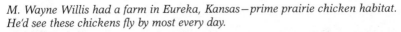

M. Wayne Willis had a farm in Eureka, Kansas — prime prairie chicken habitat. He'd see these chickens fly by most every day.

And don't think they can't. At the 1973 national running of the English springer spaniels championship in Camden, Arkansas, I watched Chuck Dryke and his co-gunners do just that. Over and over, with low-brass shells. I told Chuck his shooting was miraculous. He sluffed it off saying, "That ain't nothin'; you ought to see my son, Matt." I went to Sequim, Washington, for just that reason. I was so impressed with the lad I wrote a story in *Field & Stream* saying the Olympic committee should pick this boy up if they ever wanted to win a gold medal. They did. Matt did.

Anyway, Jim Culbertson shot, and sure enough a chicken dropped a leg and began to glide. Down the fencerow a man jumped up and ran for the bird. At the same time, Jim cast FC & AFC Keg of Black Powder for the retrieve. Because of the angles, the man beat the female Labrador retriever to the find. The poacher scooped up the bird and held it high while Powder jumped to claim her own.

Finally Jim had to stand — incidentally he was a junior college All-American football guard and retired athletic director — and walk to the pair of them. Jim said, "Give my dog the bird." The man told him, "This is my bird." Jim said, "Mister, look me over one more time." The man handed over the chicken. Isn't that a pitiful way to hunt? So Jim takes off walking the endless prairie and I tag behind. Yet, it's better than putting up with nonsportsmen who don't know rural ethics.

Jim Culbertson's penchant for hunting with Labrador retrievers (instead of just retrieving) led me to initiate the concept of the Hunting Retriever Clubs in America. Set down four Labs and you can sweep a bird field clean.

But more traditionally, any pointing dog is used for hunting the prairie chicken door-to-door, so to speak, and a retriever is needed for laying in ambush at a fencerow before a row crop field.

The Falcon Hunter

But there is another way to hunt these birds that is absolutely fascinating. A hunter can take any pointing dog and walk the prairie in hopes he'll get a point. But he must keep the dog close, and that means a lot of walking for the hunter: this prairie is endless. Better yet, launch a falcon and cast a dog to lift the chicken.

It's said a prairie chicken resembles a flying turtle with feathers. The back is all frozen together. Yet the falcon *kerwhacks!* and feathers fly and the chicken plummets to earth. If there's a flying mate with the striking falcon, this second bird comes in riding wing (as the Air Force says) and pins the prairie chicken to the ground.

To make this all the more astounding, you see a man and a gun dog standing in the field and suddenly realize this was all orchestrated by a human being. He is the falcon hunter. He has a falcon dog. And he brings game to hand with this most ancient form of hunting. To me, it is the ultimate sport: man enters nature, dupes it, controls it, and harvests it. And if the falconer were on horseback, all that he used in this sport—bird, dog, and mount—would be God-given. To me, that makes for pure sport and unequaled drama.

I'm with Steve Sherrod, Ph.D., a master falconer and director of the Sutton Avian Research Center in Bartlesville, Oklahoma, a conservation group that works on education, conservation, and research that relates to birds and their habits.

There is a new brand of dog professionals in America today. They train with intimacy, not intimidation; they are multibreed instead of single-breed trainers; and they reward with sheer love. Gary Ruppel of Elizabeth, Colorado, takes time out from a hot summer training session to rest and bond with his pointer pup. He'll do the same thing years later while hunting the hot bleaks and barrens for prairie chicken with this gun dog.

The Falcon Dog

Steve's talk is an explosion in an encyclopedia. Intense and emphatic, he says, "The reason I've always run shorthairs (he has two of them, plus an Elhew pointer) is because they've got a brain. They work with you, compared with some dogs—like a pointer—that are just bred simply to hunt, hunt, hunt. The GSP as a dog is more cooperative. They work with you and for you all the time. For my purposes, the shorthairs are one of the most intelligent bird dogs. They're not as big-running as a pointer—which is why I use the Elhew for hunting in expansive pastures. He runs big, I stop him, and release the GSP to hunt short.

"The GSP has got to do everything you tell him. It is absolutely vital. Such dogs are lifelong companions and will do anything you ask them to do. If I asked my bitch to commit suicide, that dog would do it."

Hunting the Chicken

"The ultimate falcon hunt is the prairie chicken," Sherrid says. "That's because this is a tough bird, and he's fast. He's the sportiest of them all.

"Our training season starts October 1. It's too hot for the falcons, but you get up early and try to make the best of it. I'll be out there sitting in the dark waiting for the chickens (in this case the lesser pinnated grouse) to come in. Eventually, we see a flock land in this stubblefield.

"I put the dog at heel, and I've got a cast this time (cast means two birds aloft) and the falcons are flying around now and got the chickens pinned. The chickens don't want to fly; they're lying in the stubble. I'm walking out there, and let's say I get within 75 feet of where I think the chickens are, and I send the dog in. She'll bust them this time of year, for it's still green, plus those chickens have just landed and there's little scent. Also, my dog will be working with the wind—the falconer wants a "downhill streak." Which means he will always walk and flush the birds downwind so the falcon can use the wind with it to come down and lay its blow. If I'm lucky, the dog will circle around at the last instant and come in against the wind and point, holding the birds. But if she busts them, the falcons are in position overhead.

"They'll stoop on a chicken, and probably what will happen is they'll hit it in the back and knock feathers off. But that bird will fly to the nearest fencerow, and there will be a tail chase, and then the falcons will go back up about 300 feet and wait for the chicken to move so they can go into another stoop. All the while, the dog is stopped at flush. Then I send the dog into the fencerow and tell him to knock up the chicken. And down come the falcons.

"Finally, the falcons get the chicken and claim it for their meal. The dog lays close by, waiting his turn. Then I get the falcons to climb upon my glove and give a treat to the dog. The hunt is done."

If you live in a Plains state, ask around and see who's hunting with falcons. Ask to join him, to watch him. Be respectful and quiet and stay out of the way. You'll witness the most exciting tableau in nature you've ever seen.

Cooking

No matter how I cook prairie chicken, it is delicious. But this is a finite resource. I've seen the day when Kansas had a three-day season. So when hunting this bird, respect its scanty numbers and take only one to say you've done it. Two to say you've had a meal. If you really want a taste treat, use my recipe for sage hen to cook this bird. Ginger and mustard are two flavors you can substitute for Tabasco and garlic.

15

Sharptail Grouse and Hungarian Partridge

In dawn's soft light we hunt the North Dakota prairie for sharptail grouse and Hungarian partridge. These birds are not related, but since I hunt them together I'll present them together. Matter of fact, sharptail grouse have been known to interbreed with greater pinnated grouse (prairie chicken), with whom they bear a remarkable likeness, while the Hungarian partridge (also known as Huns, or gray partridge) share many traits with the bobwhite.

SHEILA, AN ENGLISH springer spaniel import (ESS), maintains a constant beat at gun range before us: casting 20 yards right, then crossing 20 yards left. She hunts head up, searching for the bird's scent. Then her tail beat quickens, her head goes down for foot scent, and she vacuums the mixed prairie grass floor.

She's on to something.

Running to the left, she suddenly raises her head (she's deep into the birds' scent cone now and shifting back to body scent); she leaps to have the prairie erupt before her as twenty-five Huns rocket away. The birds surprise me, but springer trainer Tom Ness, of Bismarck, North Dakota, drops two, and Sheila is cast to fetch the near one.

Tom beams as he tells me, "English springer spaniels are a dense

This sharptail grouse was carved completely from wood and hand painted by Jim Pettijohn. I still look at this mount and swear it's real.

cover—a punishing-cover—dog that has to root out the bird. The pointer would point from afar. The springer digs the bird out. He'll cast into this silver buffaloberry here, and it's tangled and thorny. He'll come out all roughed up, lips bleeding, thorns stuck in his nose, but he'll not quit. He'll keep hunting."

Then Tom explains, "A pointer works for the bird, but the springer works for the gun. From the start of training, the dog learns he always finds birds close to me—I'm throwing them from my gamebag—and I make sure there are no wild birds ahead for him to stumble on. Success breeds success. I'm the bird producer; the dog gradually learns if he wants a bird he must stay close to me."

Later that day, Sheila produced both sharptails and Huns. There's not that much difference in the rise of the two species, though it is said the Hun will run before he'll fly. Is it possible Sheila just kept the pressure on so tight the Huns flew before they wanted?

The gun dog of choice is the English springer spaniel, though any veteran pointing dog can work these birds—if he's trained right. Why else would the classic gun dog pros of Dixie bring their English pointers, English setters, and Brittanies to the prairie for summer training before heading on to the fall field-trial circuit?

Flight Characteristics

Both sharptails and Huns break cover and loft in an explosion and a fairly tight grouping. Which prompts you to flock shoot – and miss. During hunting season both species are found in the same mixed prairie grass cover and row crops and weed fields, except the Hun avoids the heavy brush cover so favored by the sharptail.

The Huns

Along with the pheasant and chukar partridge, the Huns are the only successful importation of gamebirds to the United States. The Huns were first successfully transplanted in 1900 in – of all places – right near where the pheasants first took hold: the Willamette Valley of Oregon, a lush truck-garden environment with nearly daily mist. Or you might even say, rain.

The birds are named Hungarian partridge, but they were imported from Russia, Sweden, and Germany as well as Hungary. A great population of Huns resides in Central Canada. In the United States, they stretch intermittently from the state of Washington east to Michigan.

The birds weigh some 13 ounces, measure about 13 inches from bill to tail, and have a wing span of 16 inches. You will identify them on the wing by recognizing their rusty outer tail feathers: the inner tail feathers are gray. In hand, the Hun displays a brown cap and ear patch with a cinnamon face. The breast and upper belly are gray highlighted with chestnut crescents. The back is gray to brown with darker wings, which display white streaks. The female is similar, but somewhat less drab than the male.

Huns are generally associated with grassland and semidesert vegetation. For example, in Oregon, where they were first successfully released, they prefer bunch grass and sagebrush areas near cultivated crops. The Huns avoid woodlands, but can be found in brushy areas. During the winter they form a roosting circle, such as bobwhite, to keep warm and stay alert. They have the ability to burrow under snow to obtain food.

Like the Gambel's quail, the father will care for the young, and it has been noted some bachelors will try to lure chicks from haphazard parents.

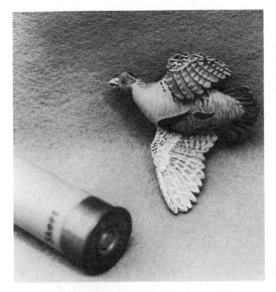

Once again, miniaturist Dick Cook has captured a gamebird in flight with this Hungarian partridge sailing past a shotgun shell. That, folks, is exactly what they look like in flight. (Photo by Dick Cook)

The Gun Dog and Huns

When detected by man or dog, the Hun takes off running, executing an erratic course to confuse his pursuer. He has a covey burst even more dynamic than a bobwhite's. Once the bird lifts, it may fly a half-mile before settling—only to run again. That's why the English springer spaniel is so valuable. This dog keeps the pressure on. He forces the Hun to take early flight, whereas a good pointing dog would point, relocate, point, relocate—or, better yet, be trained to go afield and double back to push the birds toward the gun. At any rate, there's no use following a covey in hopes of getting up singles. By the time the hunter covers the 100 to 200 yards the birds flew, the birds have run another 100 yards.

Unpredictability is the hallmark of the Hun. He will loft to a nearby hill and land on the far slope, or he will take off, land, and double back on the hunter like the pheasant. A Hun's favorite defense is to loaf on near-bare hilltops and watch for predators. However, I have jumped them from row crops, and I recall, vividly, kicking them out of 4-foot-tall sunflowers. Like pheasants, they ran to the edge—a road—when it became mandatory they loft or be dominated by the dog.

A testy target, the Hun deserves our admiration, not only for knowing the game better than we do, but also for living in sometimes marginal and even desolate land.

Sharptail Grouse

The sharptail grouse can be found – in North Dakota at least – anywhere you kick up a Hun. His territory ranges from Canada to Southern Colorado, and from northern Michigan to Oregon. The adult male
measures some 18 inches, has a wingspan of 20 inches, and weighs
about 2 pounds. He strongly resembles the greater prairie chicken,
with one exception. The sharptail has a black line that starts at the
bird's bill and runs through the eye. Cheeks and throat are white. The
belly and sides are white with black darts: the back distinguished with
black mottling. The wings are dark brown with a white pattern. He
has a yellow comb above each eye, and on each side of the neck is an
invisible air sack that can be seen only when inflated. At such time,
these sacks appear pink to pale purple. Both sexes are feathered to the
base of the toes. The white underparts are the outstanding characteristic of a sharptail in flight.

Of all the grouse, the male sharptail is the most frenzied of
dancers. He dances to assure competitors he's ready to fight, to attract
a mate, and just to advertise his display grounds. The males jump,
cackle, rattle their tails, issue a great repertoire of calls, erect their
tails, stretch their wings, and inflate their eye combs and neck sacks.

Habitat

An imperative for sharptails is brushy and woody cover with mixed
stands of hardwoods and conifers (ideally containing their favorite
tree, the aspen). The birds also require moderate cover for nesting,
roosting, and feeding. Sparse cover is favored for dusting.

The conifers and hardwoods serve as winter grounds that provide
warmth, protection, and browsing. Sharptails do not roost in trees
overnight; instead, they burrow under available snow for warmth.
However, daylight finds them flying from tree to tree in search of food.
These grouse are seed-eaters (a secondary source are greens), but in
winter they can sustain themselves on rose hips, willow buds, and
both buds and cactins of aspen and birch as well as other trees and
bushes. In the warm months, insects form a minor part of their diet.

Behavior

Like their cousins, the prairie chickens, sharptail grouse like to congregate on sparse grass hilltops to survey their surroundings. I've driven
them from these observation posts to see them go over the shoulder of
the hill and soar to the floor below. As far as I'm concerned, they loft

remarkably like Huns. However, unlike Huns, which give you an erratic flight, the sharptail bores straight ahead. Sharptails alternately beat their wings and soar, until finally they set their wings and glide to their next hide. Also, in warm weather at least, the sharptail holds for a dog better than a Hun.

Gun Dog Training Birds

Both the sharptail (and to a lesser extent, the Hun) are invaluable for gun dogs in America. They are the training birds for southern pros who head for the northern prairies each summer to fine-hone their charges. The dogs come off these two prairie birds and are immediately switched to bobwhites for the fall field-trial campaign. Plus, there are major field-trial events held in the Dakotas and Canada at the end of training season.

But there is a problem. Many people in these northern states and Canada feel the dog pros disturb the birds and cut down on population. Except for rare instances, this is not the case, but still the charges are made. Why would a dog pro destroy his only asset for summer training on wild birds?

The secret of these northern prairies is that the gun dogs run a limitless race to bluffs. These are depressions left in the land where the sand has blown out, or where the buffalo wallowed, and the water pooled (in wet years) to raise stands of wolf willows. ("Wolf Willows" is a name given these bluffs by Canadians that has caught on in North Dakota. Actually, the bluffs contain few willows, but instead, stands of aspens and several varieties of poplar trees.)

Why would the dogs want to run to these trees? Because in good years they are loaded with sharptail grouse "nooning" from the summer sun. And the beauty of sharptail grouse is that when the young are flushed in hot weather (July 1 through August 15) they make a short, twittering flight and set down quick at the first stand of grass or copse of bushes so the dog can work them again and again. Plus, they are widely scattered, so the dogs can work the singles. Constant bird contact is what the young sharptail grants the trainer.

Never on a Hot Day

Grouse enthusiasts hate to see the hunting season open on a hot day; the chickens congregate in the bluffs to avoid the heat, and the slob hunters surround the bluff with 12-gauge shotguns. There's no way these chickens can get out of there.

Once again, those young chickens that do escape fly to the nearest cover, but by now the covey is bunching. However, the mother will go farther – all the while acting as though she is crippled, a technique she has used to outwit fox.

But a cool day, the chickens leave the bluffs and, according to one native, you can't get within 400 yards of a chicken. That's an exaggeration – if it weren't, the birds could never be hunted – but his point is well made. What he's saying is this: In cool or cold weather, the bird changes. No longer is he accessible in a bluff. Instead, he is scattered on the wide prairie and is mighty elusive. He'll break at the sound of a dog whistle, a slammed car door, or a hunter's cough.

This is why the sharptail grouse is the most hunted bird on opening day in America. The hunters reappear the following weekend, but after that they generally leave this bird alone. By November few hunters try for the sharptail. However, I've hunted them in downright cold weather just following a gun dog across the prairie. Points of opportunity, if you're in the right locale, especially the badlands of North Dakota, are mulberry and wolf willow bluffs.

Where You Find Huns

Huns can be found anywhere. But generally, they are located in hedgerows, along edges where cultivated crops interchange with grass and weedfields, and at their lookout posts on hilltops.

You'll be forced to make long shots on both Huns and sharptails, so you'd better use 12-gauge models with high-brass 4s, 5s, or 6s. If you could get them close, 7½s would be your loads.

On the Grill

Both birds are delicious and can be prepared most any way to cause excitement and good reception at the table. But I've learned to take a mixed bag of these two birds and prepare them together. Let's barbecue!

The secret to barbecuing gamebirds is proper heat. The rack in your grill must be 5 inches above the coals. Test for heat by holding your hand 5 inches above the white coals; if you can keep it there 3 seconds, the fire is ready to grill. Holding your hand there 5 seconds means the fire is too cool to do any good. To increase the heat, shake the ash from the charcoals, arrange them closer together, and fan them with a bellows or newspaper. A hair dryer does this fast. To lower the temperature, disperse the coals, and douse with a spray of water.

You can find some cover for the prairie grouse. I recall hunting sharptail and Huns in a field of sunflowers that reached up to my armpits. This pointer pup has staked out a covey of Huns in a weed patch.

Okay. Remove the stems, de-seed, and finely chop 4 pickled jalapeno peppers. Mince 4 cloves garlic. Portion out 1 tsp. dry mustard and 1 tsp. each dried sweet basil and oregano, and rub to a powder. Continue apportioning 2 tsps. salt, 3 tbls. orange juice, 1/2 cup honey, 3 tbls. red-wine vinegar, 2 tbls. olive oil, 1 large minced onion, 6 tbls. catsup, and 2 tbls. Tabasco. Cut 5 pounds of sharptails and Huns into serving pieces.

Mince jalapeños and garlic. In a glass bowl, combine minced peppers, garlic, dry mustard, basil, oregano, salt, orange juice, and vinegar. Let the potion marry.

Place olive oil in a saucepan over medium heat. Add onion and sauté until onions are transparent. Stir in catsup and Tabasco, then add the salsa containing jalapeños.

Place the fowl on rack skin-side down. When black-marked by the bars of the grill, turn and grill bone-side down. Remove the fowl from the grill and cover the rack with aluminum foil. Puncture the foil with a fork to make a pattern of ventilation holes.

Place the fowl on the foil, skin-side down, and brush with barbecue sauce. Turn fowl and brush again. Continue turning for one hour. The fowl is done when a knife prick produces clear juices. Recipe serves four.

16

Puddle Ducks

Duck hunting is the most exciting sport in the world. It is endless, ageless, sexless: rich or poor, hale or lame, bright or dull, gifted or denied—a life of duck hunting belongs to everyone.

Like now. It's crisp-up, color-up, stick-'em-up time on the prairie. Fall is here. The grasses stiffen; turn gold and wine. The seeds poke whiskers into whatever passes by, hoping—like hippies used to hope—to be transported by their beards to a new life.

Early-season teal hunters arrive at stands wearing Banlon, roll-on, and insect repellent. No thermos of hot chocolate now, it's Tang. And making their way, or sitting in the shade of giant cattails, the hunters' sweat saturates their eyebrows, streaks a line down their back, and sogs their socks.

IT'S THE START of legal season, when the early birds leave their northern nesting grounds, cruising south in bluebird weather: the sun is bright, the sky is clear, and the wind is calm. Usually, we'll see the puddle ducks. These are waterfowl that tip up when feeding; they haunt shallow water, rocking forward until their bills touch food; then they force down their butts, come right-side up, and bring their morsels with them. Some also strain the water for microscopic fare with their unique bills.

M. Wayne Willis would hunt a field, stream, or pond on Sunday then return to begin painting it on Monday. Consequently, most of his paintings are of places he hunted. That's the case with these mallards. (Photo by Chromatech Corp.)

You'll see them, thousands of them, all manner of species of them, bobbing on water in every state: in weed-seed fields, in submerged timber, in flooded row crops, packing-plant slews, irrigation tailing pits. You'll find the puddle ducks anywhere that is shallow and has something to eat.

A Great Extended Family

They come in all sizes, from the diminutive teal (12 ounces) to the almost lumbering mallards (2½ pounds, 23½ inches in length, and a 36-inch average wingspan). Their family includes pintails, gadwalls, baldpates, blue-wing teal, green-wing teal, cinnamon teal, black ducks, wood ducks, and shovelers. I also include the fulvous tree duck (a rare event) as a tip-up, for they do not habitually nest in trees and prefer shallow water. These are colorful ducks that usually sport blue, white, green, red, and russet in their wing patch. And they can have novel heads, like the white crescent on a blue-wing drake or the Band-Aid patch on the throat of a wood duck drake. The pintails come in tuxedos, the mallards are zoot-suiters with fluorescent green heads, and the staid gadwall makes a fashion statement with just a touch of white on the wings.

I'll always remember the late M. Wayne Willis, my choice as one of the world's great outdoor oil artists and decoy carvers, saying, "Men are no damn good. Why, there ain't one out of 10,000 that can paint the feathers on a pintail hen." Their plumage is as delicate as old-world lace. Which means the gals, in their own way, like humans, are beautifully breathtaking.

When floating at rest, the wing tips on a puddle duck angle up from the back, just before the butt. When decoy carvers try to reproduce this, the tips always break off in rough use. Puddle ducks float arched back. And when they fly, the neck and head are considerably higher than the rear end. But some can fly: the pintail could outmaneuver Waldo Pepper. I've seen them whiffle (that's what I call it) — just drop out of a high sky in a direct fall, alternately turning left and right, side-slipping thousands of feet in seconds. When chased, the pintail will top out at 65 m.p.h.

Since these are the vegetarian ducks, they are sought for the table — no fish taste — though some divers (non-puddle ducks) are epicurean delights, as we'll see later. Get a flight of mallards daily marauding a cornfield and you've got something. You lay there in the furrows on your back and cannot shoot them away. They just keep piling in. It takes great resolve not to go berserk. A mallard on a corn diet is obsessed.

The waterfowl distribute themselves across America in their fall and winter flights by coming down four flyways. (In reality, there are also many subroutes.) They leave the North at different times due to their nature, nesting realities, and breeding dates. Early departees are just sunshine soldiers. But some black ducks, the ones called redlegs (the nickname may be due to their length of stay in the ice water or to the fact that older ducks sport distinctive red legs) will not leave their northern haunts until mad-dad wind throws iced mace in their face. Then they come like jets and bore through too often with no mind to check your decoys. For they are the wariest duck of all.

The Harvest

Puddle ducks are shot many ways. You can scull or paddle to them in a boat and shoot them as they jump; find a location where waterfowl habitually fly within gunning range, and take your stand for pass-shooting; or gun for the birds over decoys.

This gives you all kinds of shooting possiblities, but remember, everything is based on shallow water. You jump them on a farm pond by sneaking up the backside of a dam, or catch them in seed fields, weed patches, and irrigated row crops. Entice them to drop from the sky in flooded timber by hugging a tree and kicking the water with your booted foot so the waves make the decoys bob. Or, in the case of wood ducks, you can course the river banked with heavy timber – either afoot or floating on the water – to jump-shoot the ducks as they're surprised by your coming around each bend. Best of all, you can decoy them and blow a duck call to entice them. You do this from a blind ashore, or while in a sneak boat, layout boat, or stake blind at sea. Now you're hunting.

For novelty, you can train a tolling dog that will frolic on the bank and entice the ducks to come near him to see just what his antics are all about.

Celebrated decoy carver Joe Wooster of Ashley, Ohio, and his Lab, Happy, hunt a forest stream for wood ducks. Joe is glassing far downstream to see if any woodies are resting. Someone once asked Joe what he did for a living. When Joe said he carved decoys, the person countered, "Couldn't find real work, huh?"

A group of Savannah, Tennessee, good-ol'-boys toss mallard decoys in a honey hole surrounded by flooded timber. An old Lab sits in the boat and ponders when he'll have to hit water for a fetch.

The Decoy

A decoy is a floating, polychromatic sculpture of the bird you intend to take, though most birds will flock to the standard mallard drake. Heck, on the Platte River I've shot them coming into 1-gallon gas cans painted black. All you really need is something to float and imitate duck life.

But the purists get busy, as with confidence decoys. Hunters observed how wily the blue heron is, for example. So they buy one, or carve one, and stick him up nearby to give the incoming ducks a false sense of security. Big-water hunters display a herring gull decoy on the bow of their punt or sneak skiff.

Other purists want every feather carved on the duck.

The old market gunners set the standard, though. No nonsense, just a good silhouette and roundness, a low head so the duck wouldn't look like it was suddenly startled, and the right weight and keel construction to keep it floating steady.

Oh sure, rivers that iced up called for decoys with high breasts so the decoys wouldn't go under. Choppy water, like Lake Michigan, called for big plate-shaped decoys. Modern hunters opt for lightweights. Some decoys are made of a thin rubber material (called Deeks) with a wire diaphragm on the bottom. Hold the decoy straight out, drop it, have it capture air, and seal the diaphragm on the water. You can carry fifty of them.

All decoys must be arranged in a raft. They must funnel ducks to your gun. And you are in a hide. So all manner of configurations have been tried. What I like best is a broad V. I'm at the point of the V in my blind, with two arms going out. For example, one arm runs north and one runs south, and I shoot west to avoid the morning sun. Ducks going in either direction have an arrow of decoys to follow to my stand. My second choice for a decoy configuration is a fish hook, with the shank downwind and the hook making a pool before my blind. The ducks will follow the long line to the waiting pool.

The ducks are not going to land on your blind, but in a pool between the decoys. You'll never find a bird just flop in close to another bird (except redheads; they like to pile up). They keep their distance. So here they all come, piling in to the honey hole, as we call it, with decoys stretching out at an angle from them on either side. You hold your breath as their wings cup the air, legs adangle, their heads craned forward for a better look, their backs arched. *Wham!* They're yours.

Jeff Devazier, the Chesie trainer, launches a bold leaper for a downed duck. The dog sits on a deer treestand (visible behind the Chesie) until Jeff orders him to fetch.

First There Was the Wind

But remember the wind. Always the wind. Ducks are wind birds. They always land into the wind. So, if the wind were blowing into your blind, would the ducks maneuver behind you and come in over your hide to land? False hope. But with the broad V going north or south, the ducks can come in from either direction—then land north into the wind or south into the wind. Or they can come in at an angle and turn into a wind that's blowing across the blind from the hunter's back.

They rise the same way, always turning to take the wind and lofting to cup it in their wings.

Don't ever forget the wind.

The Retriever

Now for the duck dog: the retriever, which is any dog that will retrieve. He's in the blind with you, either hidden or right out in the open. Some say an exposed dog will spook ducks. Bosh. How do they account for the success of the tolling dogs?

I like to have the dogs out where they can see . . . and I can see them. The veteran gun dog will save you many ducks. Ducks can see the flash of your facial skin, but the dog's face is fur. Let the dog look up, and you monitor his eyes. Those eyes—or his thumping tail or his soft whine—will tell you exactly where the birds are and what they are doing.

Keep a well-drained place for the dog to rest. He's wet; let it drip off and not make him puddle in it. And when he launches for retrieves, don't have the decoy cords so long on your set that he gets tangled up. In this case, two things go wrong. First, he drags the decoys to sea and ruins your layout; second, late-arriving ducks see the dog in tow with a duck and wonder what the hell's going on. They leave you without decoying, and that's bad. You want every opportunity—whether you shoot or not—for the test of the hunt is in the tricking, not the taking.

Retrievers fetch marks and blinds. A mark is any bird the dog has seen fall. A blind is a bird the dog has not seen fall. But you have, and now you must direct the dog to the fetch by whistle and hand signals. You cast with the command, "Back," with one whistle blast meaning stop. Blow the whistle, the dog turns about in the water, paddles, and you give him a hand signal to go back, left, right, or come in. The dog complies—if trained.

Beware of dogs clambering on shelf ice. They do so by curling their bodies like a shrimp, edging their elbows on the ice shelf, and

"Willoughby's Pride" by Lou DePaolis of North Syracuse, New York, is the best painting of a working Lab I've ever seen. It's been a long day and the dog moseys along, thinking deeply. I've seen this expression from a duck blind a thousand times.

convoluting themselves up. I've never seen a dog drown. But I've seen some Herculean struggles. As I once wrote:

> *Then it was done—fast as begun.*
> *With Herculean stroke the hold he broke*
> *Of the ice water's strangle with the big drake adangle,*
> *And came for me crawling, o'er the frozen mud's galling.*

His coat dripped ice like grains of rice,
His white muzzle locked from the grip of the shock,
The flag of his tail drug flat on the trail;
The old Lab was dying, I was kneeling, and crying.

Cattails reeded from the wind a dirge to fit the scourge
That nature meted out. And then the bout
Saw Death the victor, but not before he licked her,
For death couldn't stop him handing

> *me the bird as he was standing.*

On bluebird days, you need no special provisions for the retriever. But when the wind blows blue and the snow swirls and ice sizzles, get the dog a straw bed and let him crowd close to your safety stove. After a retrieve in such stuff, you can rough him up with straw. He'll thank you for it.

Put your ducks away. Dogs like to fondle them. Have the dog on the job, not licking some duck.

If you've got really severe conditions, don't insist your retriever be a field-trial perfectionist. Instead of casting him 300 yards out and angled down the lake for a duck, walk him along the bank, get even with the floating duck, and cast him straight out. We're not after blue ribbons here, but meat on the table.

If your dog can't see the duck, help him. Throw shell casings, pebbles, or apple cores at the thing. Get a splash. And when the dog is after a strong cripple, lay off. Let him have his head and his way. I've had dogs gone two hours after a strong wing-shot diving duck. It's rough. The dog twirls and peers, strains and dives, and the bird submerges only to bob up 20 feet away. So always try to shoot dead. If the dog is far enough away from a surfacing cripple, try to finish it off: though I admit shooting a duck on the water is like trying to pierce armor.

Get out of the blind once in a while and cast the dog down shore. Let him run in the tall grass, even spook up a rabbit, quail, or pheasant. Give him hamburger balls or $1/4$-ounce capsules of honey to keep up his energy and his blood sugar.

There's no getting around deafness in old retrievers. They're just under the gun. You must wear earplugs, but the dog—God bless him. You can do best by getting your muzzle completely outside the blind before firing. The blind material can muffle the retort.

Dogs can't work with stool on their mind. Clean your dog out on the walk to the blind.

And before moving on, I'd like to make a final gun dog reference. There is a retriever specialist who is an absolute delight. That's the American water spaniel that was developed to ride in a Dan Kidney boat (an heirloom today, if you have one), leap from the bow to make his retrieves, and be paddled or sculled through flooded grass flats. He's a delight at home and an inspiration afield. We all know of the Chesapeake Bay retrievers, the goldens, and the Labs. I just thought this little specialist from Wisconsin deserved mention.

I was staying with Bill Koelpin, an award-winning sculptor, carver, and painter of Wauwatosa, Wisconsin, when I noticed a bronze still in the wax of a hard-put duck hunter and an American water spaniel at the whim of the wind and a white-capped marsh. In a split second I said, "Damn the wind." And that's what Bill named the piece.

The Firing Line

And now for guns.

The duck harvester is the field-grade, 12-gauge Remington model 1100 automatic, with a 30-inch barrel, plugged to three shells and loaded with two 6s and a final-firing 4 for taking the getaway bird. We want this in a modified or full-choked barrel. But I must admit, I've

The bronze, "Damn the Wind," depicts artist Bill Koelpin and his American water spaniel caught in a gale on Wisconsin's Horicon marsh. (Photo by Mark Deprez)

Don't underestimate this American water spaniel with the outrageous hairdo. He's Hawkins, the dog riding out the wind in Bill Koelpin's "Damn the Wind."

seen more waterfowl taken with a Winchester Model 12 than with any other gun.

I always shoot high-brass shells for waterfowl. I just want the extra power – especially now with the legal requirement of steel shot. Steel penetrates very poorly, so you must be on the duck with a direct and slam-bang blast to bring him down. I want no cripples on my pond. I recently scored a direct hit with No. 4s on a Canada goose not 30 yards from the blind. The impact knocked the bird sideways; he missed one wing beat, and soared on. No. 4s in lead would have brought him crashing to the water.

The Groaning Board

Not everyone likes duck, but those who do are fanatics. Some say it tastes too wild or tastes like liver. I know I've eaten a ton of them – as I say – baked in aluminum foil drowned in Coca Cola, and I enjoyed every bite. But to do it right – when you have the time – remove the backbone and brush both sides of the bird with butter. Broil bone side to heat. Grill duck 10 minutes, then turn for 12 minutes, or until you're satisfied. Salt and pepper as you like. Serve with a bottle of Tabasco, french fries, and cooked broccoli smothered with melted cheese.

If you have more time, the following recipe makes up an epicurean's delight. It comes from Gloria and Jim Pettijohn.

Slice two duck breasts in strips. Gather ¼-stick butter or margarine, 1 tbls. Worcestershire sauce, 1 tbls. red currant jelly, 1 cup brandy, 2 tbls. triple sec liqueur. Melt butter, Worcestershire, and currant jelly in skillet. Add burgundy and liqueur. Add duck. Salt and pepper. Simmer 20 to 30 minutes. You can thicken the sauce with cornstarch in a little cold water.

Year-Round Dedication

In closing, I want to emphasize that duck hunting is year-round. You must practice with the gun, train the dog, build the boat, weave the blind, perfect the call, paint the decoys, scout the area, find the summer nests, go to the decoy shows and duck tournaments, read the literature, and haunt the gun dog stores.

What's life to a hunter without a new dream for some piece of equipment? Trying out a new gun at the range, going to meet call makers, visiting decoy carvers. Following the want ads in the impossible hope you'll find an antique decoy for nothing. Learning who your outdoor writers and outdoor artists and game wardens are and cultivating their friendship. Learn their craft, get insight into their problems, become a helping hand.

A German shorthaired pointer shows his zest on a water retrieve for a puddle duck.

I'll never forget the time I flew all the way to Chicago to call on Harold Hartael of Dundee, Illinois, generally considered to be the premier decoy carver of the last half of the twentieth century. We talked. He was kind. We struck it off. And when I was leaving to fly 2,000 miles back home, he handed me a shoe box with a slight heft to it. I said, "What's this?" and he replied, "Oh, it's a pied-billed grebe I carved for some king, but I think you'd enjoy it more than him."

There are some great people in the great outdoors. Get to know them.

And remember how to hunt Tarrant—if I may be permitted that phrase. What I'm thinking about now are those bluebird days when the ducks weren't flying at the 19,857 acres of Cheyenne Bottoms, located in Kansas, or the Mallard Gun Club, or the Hoisington Gun Club, just north of the bottoms, where Jim Culbertson and I used to hunt ducks so much. We'd get out of the blind and walk the north bank, kicking the mud for old-time market gunner decoys. We found them by the ton. Who thought they'd ever become valuable? As I say, it just pays to hunt the Tarrant way. Forget trying to get your limit; just have fun in the field for the day. Open all your senses, and try to absorb everything from the scum on the pond to the spider web floating on the soft air.

17

Divers, Geese, and Brant

Now come the legendary birds of the black-powder bar-
rage and the first vigilant conservation press, the wing-
whistlers who can hit (some say) 95 m.p.h. riding the blast
of an ice-pelting northern. The divers.

The great birds who haunt wide expanses of water,
even seas and oceans. The master flyers, deep divers, and
uncanny lead carriers: yes, these are the birds that fly
away with their hearts shot out. It's an old claim.

This bird and the market gunner were wed in history:
the grisly multigun shooter in his hazardous sink box with
maybe 500 decoys, the birds coming in long and seemingly
endless skeins, and the merciless guns blasting after the
birds sat and bunched — and before they could lift — and
their dead bodies floated belly up on the chopped water to
the waiting sloop that hauled them aboard and delivered
them fresh or salted to an insatiable Eastern hotel and
cafe market.

A DIVING DUCK hangs heavy in the hand; it has a low center of gravity, a unique density. I don't say these things as a game biologist: I don't even come close. I'm just a hunter. And that's how these ducks feel to me. Like the way the feathers lay. Not like a puddle duck. The feathers are tight and close-laid and interknit. Try to shoot through them, as with a cripple. You'll see. The birds are tough and they are sleek.

All divers are flying missiles. They come over your blind with the crack of a jet, make a far sliding turn, and buzz you again and again. These canvasbacks by M. Wayne Willis are sizzling the air above a stream. [Photo by Chromatech Corp.]

These ducks are built for flight—fast flight. Ever have a laughing flock of blackjacks (ring-neck ducks) jab at your blind? Like a grade-school bully slapping your face on alternate sides twenty times before you can break free and run backwards. That's the way they hit a blind: zip left, then right, ripping the sky, sliding on the far turns. Yes, there's nothing that can fly like a diver.

Nor does anything appear with such bounty. You can have them hit you by the hundreds. Especially at sea. A fortune in decoys surrounding you. All divers. Mostly drake decoys to show the white of their plumage. But black enough so the ducks know they aren't the small whitecaps of waves.

You also may come upon the ducks rafting, taking the sun, or dozing after a meal. These ducks eat both animal and vegetable matter. A select fare are sought because they dine on buds of wild celery, for example, and they come to the table as good as any corn-fed puddle duck.

But as I started to say, you're now in a sneak boat or a sculled punt (usually gray or bedecked with natural grasses). The ducks see this formless object moving, but no ostensible movement, no man. Then you raise up and fire as they loft and strive to get away.

Finally, there are those boats where your feet are covered with a domed deck, and you lie in wait on your back: a Barnegat Bay boat. I've ridden them on Lake Erie only to conclude you've got to start gunning that way when you're a kid to ever get the hang of it. And you raise up when the birds come over and take your pass shots. Or you're in a ten-second-rigged stand of reed, debris, driftwood, and grass where you wait your fortune in the salt flats or on the shore.

Above all, divers are hazardous-water ducks: they live in the coastal areas and tidal basins with chopped water, swells, waves, treacherous tides, and floating ice—even though their favorite haunts are shallow bays like Pamlico Sound. You can get an approximation of it—as I have—by shooting the side waters of the Mississippi River in its middle tributary south of New Orleans in a pirogue, an imagination of a boat that shudders to the currents, tips on its occupant's breathing, and rocks on firing. You'd better part your hair in the middle to hunt out of this mustang. And with a retriever on board, you've just handed him your life.

I've hunted the coasts, bays, capes, and sounds, plus inland there

The Lab in Bill Koelpin's deep sea bronze looks back for a shoreline that disappeared a long time ago. [Photo by Chromatech Corp.]

have been the storied puddle duck ricefields of Stuttgart, Arkansas, the milofields of Colorado and Kansas, even the Salt River in the Sonoran desert. I've dusked the birds over bait in Great Britain, shot them at night in Germany, and tried to hit them as they hurtled on a high wind down an East Indian gorge. I've spooked them from a host of ricefields in the Orient, chased them across Europe, and nearly frozen to death waiting for them in Scandinavia.

Waterfowl have always been my bird, and I want them wild: never from a game reserve tower. Their coursing the earth, defying the elements, conquering land, air, and water, and living self-sufficiently have always peaked my pride for them, and my admiration. I've sought them more places than I can recall.

Diver Behavior

Expect the diver to hit your puddle duck blind. He will. And often. You'll need not look up to tell who cometh. When the diver goes by there can be a wind whistle. And when he turns back, and his mind is made up, he won't whiffle from a height, but like a hot jet landing, fly right into your decoys just skimming the water. He hits with a cascading splash and scoots forward. He lands faster than a puddle duck, but he lofts slower, pattering along the water to get airborne. The puddle duck can fly up the inside of a smokestack; it takes the diver a runway to rise.

Species

There are many diving ducks. They include the redhead, canvasback, ring-neck, greater and lesser scaup, American and Barrows goldeneye, bufflehead, old squaw, Steller's eider, northen eider, American eider, Pacific eider, king eider, spectacled eider, white-winged scoter, surf scoter, American scoter, and the mergansers, which we don't shoot.

The Ruddy Duck

Finally, there's the ruddy duck, which is unique to all American Anatidae. It is a small bird with chunky body and round wings. It flies in knots where you can get six birds in one or two shots. It is distributed from coast to coast, and has the distinction of a tail that can be raised at a 90-degree angle like a displaying prairie chicken. It approximates the grebe in its swimming, diving, and flying peculiarities. Watch for a small duck flying rapidly and very close to the water. They'll buzz your decoys in a straight line at 6 feet off the water.

Distinctions of the Divers

With a few unique exceptions, diving ducks are not spectacularly colored. The canvasbacks and redheads with their brilliant, gleaming red heads are the rare event. I see divers as mostly black-and-white ducks. That would be their field identification. In hand, they would reveal subtle contrasts and contradictions.

A diving duck flies with his tail higher than a puddle duck, and he seems to be shorter as well, like the way a bulldog seems compact and short-coupled. All females are drab gray, brown, black, or rust. The most splendid of these birds are the eiders, with stark white backs, pastel heads, eye patches, and masks. But a midwesterner could hunt all his life and never see one of these coastal commuters.

No doubt some divers have a strong taste. A few are flat impossible to bring to the table. Just too fishy. Forget the mergansers. But get the right species on the right underwater grasses and you've got something. Hopefully, your harvest will have been on wild celery, sago pondweed, bushy pondweed, redhead grass, widgeon grass, or eel grass if its been reestablished in your waters.

Except for the everyday occurrence of divers decoying to your puddle-duck decoys, and some jump-shooting and pass-shooting, you're just not going to be using a retriever to help bring this bird to hand.

Layout boats, stake blinds, sneak boats (either paddled or sculled), and so forth just don't generally accommodate a dog. The market gunners were dogless; their boats were too small and treacherous to handle a dog. The serious market gunner had downwind crews pick up his ducks. Only an individual shooting from shore or from a blind in a bay, sound, or river could effectively use a dog.

The Gun Dog

And that dog would be a Chesapeake Bay retriever. I'll give you one example. In the early 1930s, retriever field trials were just catching on in America. Long Island was the initial seat of contest. One Saturday, a field-trial crowd was in the first water series fetching ducks from the water when Chesapeake Dilwyne Montauk Pilot came to the line. This was a burly, tight-curled, copper-colored monster with a penchant for ice flows and white-capped water.

Pilot was cast for the last of his two ducks. The duck went to sea. Pilot pursued. The field-trial crowd moved on and ran a land series and was coming back to water when, lo and behold, here comes Pilot, after two hours asea, fetching the duck.

The judges said, "He's out of the trial. He missed the land series."

The crowd, however, rightfully replied, "No, he's not out. He just won the trial. That's exactly what we're testing the dogs for." Pilot was a Chesie.

This doesn't mean other bona fide retrievers can't do it all as well. They can. Like the national open trial years ago at Saint Louis when the river froze and they kept motorboats going to clear a fetching hole. Goldens, Labs, and Chesies all could handle the misery.

But back to the Chesies. They are a unique dog, usually a one-man animal; loyal, courageous, defensive, and possessive of their owner and all his property. Thus, the market gunner who would put up with a dog and had a punt large enough to accommodate him could pull his rig ashore and leave his gun, decoys, and ducks aboard while he went to his house to eat or pick up something at the store. When he came back, there'd be nothing missing.

Pity the poor soul who would approach such an idle rig. Critics say the dog is aggressive, admirers say he's possessive. Either way, the dog can get any duck that falls in any type of water under any conditions, and make sure you get the bird home.

The Gun

Coastal-water duck hunters have a heritage of large guns. Punt gunners had ought gauge; guns that weighed over 100 pounds and fired more than 1 pound of shot. Today's gunners prefer 12 or 10 gauges, bored modified or full. There are just some long shots one sometimes has to make. Of course, they're all shooting steel shot now, and that calls for heavier loads.

Geese

Finally, we must mention the geese. They are the ultimate of all game-birds. The bombers who drive men mad—remember at the front of the book the guy in the pickup truck that stole the goose from Jim Culbertson? There's just something about a goose.

The Canadas are the prize: of which there are many subspecies. But when I speak of Canadas I mean the Canada maximus, the giant Canadas. Ornithologists who catch a flock of these birds in a net will average out the old and young and tell you the bird weighs 13.6 pounds. Phew! Redwing Tavern is just north of Cheyenne Bottoms near Hoisington, Kansas, where each year the largest geese are brought in and weighed to vie for a biggest-goose prize. My memory

A Canada goose and gander tend to their hatch; can you see the little ones to the left of Mother?

tells me the largest goose brought to the scales was 23 pounds. Jim Culbertson and I posted many a 21-pounder. I'm talking about a big bird.

Where to Hunt

You hunt Canada geese over decoys in a land-based pit blind, in something erected along shore, or out in a sneak punt or layout boat. You also can use stickup decoys in a damp, winter wheatfield where you've dug a pit and you take them as they come into feed. Corn, milo, or any row crop will also draw Canadas. The birds are like mallards in not heeding shot over corn. They have a lust for the gold.

The Gun

You shoot them with the biggest gun you got and the heaviest load; however, No. 4 will take them. But not always in steel.

The dog is of value only in fetching this bird—a Herculean task if the goose is crippled and has gone to sea. The bird will fight the dog, flailing him with his wings. And I'm talking about wings spreading 76 inches. The bird can peck, too. He is formidable.

How to Hunt

My great delight in Canada hunting is working the call. I mean we set up a chatter, every man in the blind blowing a mouth call as well as shaking a rubber device that *Car-runnnnks*. The more the better, literally throwing up a cacophony of delirium. Then the Canadas will respond, they will beat toward your layout, if . . .

But that "if" is predictable. Most Canadas are found on preserves. Each morning they lift and head for a grainfield they probably frequented the day before. Unless you're right on the nearest firing line, you have no chance of scoring on these birds: and here you're skybusting.

No, it's after the feed, and you've hunted ducks all morning (your goose decoys are off to one side of your duck layout), and the Canadas are heading back to the preserve. That's when you can waylay them. Especially the very old and the very young who may be tired from a long flight. They'll cut their trip short and land for you.

So you call and call, finally convincing the flight to decoy. But

Decoy carver Joe Wooster sits in the back of a duck boat filled with Canada decoys off Fire Island, just minutes from Manhattan.

harken; stop your calling when the birds are some 200 yards out or they'll flare and go on. This is imperative.

You'll be greatly aided by high, heavy head winds and harsh weather that will convince the tired birds to cut their trip short.

Or you can go hunting for the Canadas in the row-crop fields where they feed, but that is a fool's endeavor. Only time I ever connected this way was by accident. I was driving by and saw them land, and I was able to sneak close enough to shoot. But remember, these birds post a sentinel who remains ever vigilant while the flock eats. He'll tell them you're there, and away they'll go.

Youth has its stupid excesses. How I recall the mud on elbows and knees while I cradled my gun in my arms as I crawled on my belly over a wet winter wheat field trying to get a shot at Canadas. The sentinel always caught me; let's face it, farmers don't plant wheat fields on rolling terrain where you can sneak the hollows. Wheat farmers want land as flat as a billiard table, and the sentinel goose can see forever.

But there are always exceptions. I've shot Canadas secreted along a barbed-wire fence. They just chanced along. And I've pond-jumped them. And laid in the weeds beside a flowing river and caught them coursing through. One morning I was hunting an 18-acre pond that had a concrete dam. I shot two mallards and the sound bounced off the dam to raise a small flight of Canadas that had spent the night there. They wanted to get away from the resounding shot, so they bore straight toward me. It was my first double. With Canadas you just never know.

Specklebellies and Snows and Blues

There are two other geese important to the hunter. They are the specklebelly and the snows and blues. The specklebellies respond to a high pitched *Car-runnnnk*, and you can call them right into the blind. They won't flare from the call like the Canadas. You can't describe this on paper, but with the specklebelly call there's a distinct break between the *Car-* and the *-runnnnk*. You'll have to hear the birds to know.

Specklebellies are wherever you find Canadas and the same rules apply.

The snows and blues are different, however. You find a bounty of these birds in south Texas, where you hunt them with any manner of ruses. I've been afield where men flew white kites and reeled in the line to bring the snows and blues to the gun. I've seen white balloons tethered among the decoys to simulate movement. It worked. I've even

A Texas snow goose hunter with his Lab arranges patches of white cloth to serve as decoys.

seen men in white coats stand and beat their arms to resemble giant birds, and sure enough, the snows and blues responded. There's a reason for this movement. Hunters lease fields and leave their decoys out. The geese fly in to be shot. So they avoid stationary decoys. But put some movement in the set, and the geese will once again think their live counterparts are feeding and come in.

But the secret to being successful on snows is picking the field you scouted the birds using the day before and setting up in the exact spot they occupied. Snow geese are homers almost to the inch. They'll pick a feed field and return day after day till it's eaten to a nub. Or take a holding pond where they rest. I know a farmer who one summer moved a 20-acre pond a half-mile across his section. That fall, here come the snow geese to land in the pond they'd used the winter before. Setting their wings, they glided to dust, crashed, then walked around in dazed wonder. From the air, they could see where the pond had been moved, but never that winter did they use the transplanted pond.

This doesn't mean you can't break the snows' routine. You can shoot 'em from a field, but more than that, a storm front can alter their flight lanes, change their feeding grounds, their holding ponds. Hunting snow geese, like any quarry, is a thinking endeavor.

This isn't a bird that's called all that much. It's the decoys that attract them. And what of the decoys? Would you believe scattered newspapers, diapers, Kleenex, paper towels? Yes, they all work. This is not the wariest of birds. Matter of fact, I was hunting with a camera one morning and the nearby hunters (I didn't know them) chided me, saying, "How do you cook that film?" And another offered, "Maybe that camera's all he knows how to shoot?" I said, "Lend me a gun." Then I walked across the field in the direction the birds were coming. A blue goose spied me and beat his wings directly to me. I shot once, he dropped like a rock, and I was able to go back to my camera with no further comments.

And why do I call the same bird a snow and blue? For that's the way they come. Some white, some blue, but they are the same bird. It's just another oddity of nature.

Jim Culbertson, the full-bore hunter, and I found these snow geese over cattle in northeast Kansas. When asked if we could hunt on his land, the farmer exclaimed, "My God yes . . . those geese are eating me out of house and home."

A solitary emperor goose at Bob Whele's Alabama kennels has fallen in love with its image in a shiny hubcap. Start the car, and the goose runs alongside, looking at its spinning likeness. Although emperor geese seldom leave Alaska, they can be found along the northern coast of California.

The Brant

And now for brant. These are ocean birds hunted essentially in bays where you can find eel grass. Just take a boat out to a sandbar and set up. Usually this is a three-man endeavor: two men hunting and a third in a pickup boat tending the deadfall. You call brant with your mouth, and they soar to your set before a layout boat or along the shoreline. Two guys can get to going with a sort of *dddddruunnnn*. The birds make a very distinctive sound, a kind of metallic, resonating, nasal tone. When they're above you, the sound always surprises you.

Body booting is a unique way of hunting these birds, but only for the young, the bold, and the physically fit. In the old days, that meant wearing a pair of chest waders and standing on the sand amidst your decoys in the bay. But the technique has progressed past that. First, there came the wet suits like scuba divers wear; now we have dry suits you can don over wool underwear and keep warm. The hunter crouches down with a hand on his gun, which floats on rafts secured between decoys. This sport is really rough on equipment: it just trashes a shotgun. So you take the gun to the shower with you when you're finished and flush it out and off with hot water. You must rid it of the damaging salt.

For the Table

A very effective way to both preserve and cook Canadas, speckle-bellies, snows/blues, and brant is to half-freeze the bird so you can thin-slice it and use the meat for wok meals or teriyaki.

If you want something unique and delicious, take two brant breasts, bone and skin them, and cut into ³/₄-inch sections. Arrange 1 onion cut into thin slices, 1 tsp. olive oil, 2 tsps. ground cumin, 2 cans chicken broth, 1 package frozen whole kernel corn, ³/₄-cup pi-

Snow geese often promenade.

cante sauce, dice 1 small red and 1 small green bell pepper, 2 tbls. cornstarch, 2 tbls. water, and 1½ cups shredded Monetery Jack cheese.

Cook the brant and onion in an oiled, heavy-duty pot. Sprinkle with cumin. Add the broth, corn, and picante sauce. Bring to a boil and immediately reduce heat. Cover and simmer 5 minutes. Ladle into soup bowls and cover with cheese. Makes six servings.

Another Definition of Hunting

There are many stories I could tell you about diver and goose hunting. The miraculous shots made, the peril of finding yourself fogged in and night falling, the tide that catches you offshore, the dog that's pushed downriver before the force of an ice flow, the tediousness in laying out 100 or so decoys. But none of them bears the true meaning of hunting that I established in the front of this book. No. Hunting is not just shooting. Remember, I said you could prove that with a tin can. You didn't need a bird. Hunting is fitting into nature, conserving your quarry, loving the out-of-doors, and seeking the beauty that can be man, dog, and bird.

There is a story that represents all I stand for, and it's told not by me, but by Bill Parton, who went quail hunting with us.

Bill was hunting in Baja California – here, let him tell it.

"A hunter comes closer to the simplicity that all of us crave inside when hunting on tidal water. For you feel the rhythm and the flow of the bay and you see the colors of the day.

"One of the most beautiful sights I've ever been granted came while hunting brant on the tidal bay at San Quintan in Baja California. There you'll find an old mill called Molina Viejo made of the volcanic rock that pockmarks the area. Consequently, it has the same color as the hills surrounding the bay. The mill is testimony to an English colony's failure, built on land given to them by the Mexican government in the nineteenth century.

"Alongside the mill are the little shacks of the fishermen who work the Sea of Cortez. There's a channel that pierces the land like a dagger and comes far enough inland to run alongside the length of the mill. And all the fishermen's overturned boats are lined up there to await the next day.

"We were hunting black brant and had brought our birds in to be cleaned. The Mexicans are very poor and seek this work. Why, their shacks are made of driftwood, scavaged plywood, old soda pop signs. They have nothing.

Bill "Web" Parton sculpts in wax the Chesie at his knee. Bill's San Quintan brant story prompts me to say, "That's hunting!"

"We gave the brant to one of the older women who lived in the line of shacks. We went ahead with the chores of the hunt, stowing our decoys, draining water from the bilge, and trailering the boat. I looked up to see this old woman and a very young granddaughter cleaning the birds on the bow of an overturned pongo [fishing dory]. She had an ancient knife, filed too many times, and she would whack off the head of each bird and leave the knife sticking in the wood.

"Her granddaughter was gleefully pulling handfuls of white breast feathers out of the ebony-colored birds. And with absolute wonder this little girl, who had nothing, thrust up her hand, high into the slip stream of air that dropped down low against the water and blew out to the open bay.

"She would shriek with delight as she opened her small brown hand and watched the explosion of pearl white down catch the wind and flow down into the open water and fuse with the light of the sun. I'll never forget. The stream of wind came down over the crumbled stone walls of the mill and over the little girl and hit the channel water and followed it to sea. And the down as far as I could see was disappearing in a thousand diamonds of light."

That's hunting!

I hope you're hunting, too.

Index

Acme, 60
African Game Trails, 78
Alabama, 40
Alamuchy, New Jersey, 28
Albany, Georgia, 48
Alberta, Canada, 99
American cocker spaniels, 12
American eiders, 159
American goldeneyes, 159
American scoters, 159
American water spaniels, 12
  ducks and, 152
Ames Plantation, 53, 55–56
Arizona, 65–71, 73–79, 81–85, 99, 100,
  109, 126
Arkansas, 5, 63–64, 130, 159
Arkansas River, 6
AyA side-by-side shotgun, 76

Bailey, John, 48–49
Baja California, Mexico, 88, 95, 99,
  169–70
Baldpates, 144
"Bandito" (Llewellyn setter), 65, 66,
  70–71
Barrows goldeneyes, 159
Bartlesville, Oklahoma, 131
Beretta Golden Snipe shotgun, 115
Berlat, Bill, 75–79
Bismarck, North Dakota, 134
Bismuth Cartridge Co., 16
Black ducks, 144, 145

Blinds
  ducks and, 146, 148, 149, 151, 154,
    155, 157, 159
  geese and, 162–64
Blue grouse, 104
  dogs for hunting, 107–8, 111
  guns for hunting, 110
  how to cook, 111–12
  how to hunt, 107–11
  how to identify, 111
  where to find, 109–11
Boats
  brant and, 167
  ducks and, 146, 147, 152, 154,
    157–58, 160, 161
  geese and, 162
Bobwhite quail, 20, 31, 68, 71, 73, 75,
  79, 87, 93, 99, 100, 104, 111, 113,
  118, 119, 121, 134, 136, 137, 139
  dogs for hunting, 44, 45, 52, 53, 57–63
  how to cook, 55–57
  how to hunt, 57–64
  how to identify, 53–55
  shooting distance for, 17
  where to find, 44–55, 57, 62–64,
    74, 81
Boots
  for dogs, 19, 77, 96
  for hunters, 24
"Brandy" (Brittany spaniel), 114
Brant, 169–70
  how to cook, 168–69

how to hunt, 167–68
  where to find, 167
British Columbia, Canada, 99, 109
Brittany spaniels, 11
  grouse and, 104, 114, 136
  partridge and, 136
  pheasant and, 41–42
  quail and, 61–63, 90
  woodcocks and, 119
Brown, David E., 72
Browning shotguns, 68, 89
  Superposed, 38
Bryan, Jimmy, 55–56
Buffleheads, 159

Calcagni, David, 119
California, 28, 87–91, 95, 99, 105, 113
California quail, 94
  dogs for hunting, 89
  guns for hunting, 89
  how to cook, 89
  how to hunt, 89, 90
  how to identify, 87
  where to find, 87–88, 90
Camden, Arkansas, 130
Camp Verde, Arizona, 78–79
Canada, 28, 99, 105, 109, 113, 136,
  138, 139
Canada geese, 161–64, 168–69
Canvasbacks, 159, 160
Carbondale, Colorado, 96, 107, 109
Chesapeake Bay retrievers, 12, 83
  ducks and, 152, 160–61
Cheyenne Bottoms (Kansas), 6, 155,
  161–62
China birds. *See* Ring-necked pheasant
Chukar partridge, 92, 136
  boots for hunting, 24
  dogs for hunting, 97, 98
  how to cook, 100
  how to hunt, 96–98, 100
  how to identify, 100
  where to find, 96, 98, 99
Cimarron River, 44
Clothing, 23–25
Clumber spaniels, 12
Cocker spaniels
  American, 12
  English, 12, 42–43
  pheasant and, 42–43
Coffeeville, Mississippi, 48
Cohen, Aaron, 78
Collars, dog, 18–20, 58
Colorado, 96, 99, 104, 105, 107–9, 127,
  138, 159

Corvallis, Oregon, 27
Culbertson, Jim, 33–34, 129, 130, 155,
  161, 162
Cumbres, New Mexico, 81–82
Curly-coated retrievers, 12

Daniel, Bud, 54
Davenport, Iowa, 5
Decoys
  brant and, 168
  ducks and, 145–49, 154–55, 157,
    159–61
  geese and, 162, 164–66
Denny, Owen, 27
"Dilwyne Montauk Pilot" (Chesapeake
  Bay retriever), 160–61
Diving ducks, 145
  how to hunt, 156–59
  how to identify, 159–60
Doves, 15
  dogs for hunting, 123–25
  guns for hunting, 126
  how to cook, 126
  how to hunt, 122–26
  how to identify, 121–22
  where to find, 121–23
Dryke, Chuck, 130
Dryke, Matt, 130
Ducks, 15
  American eiders, 159
  American goldeneyes, 159
  American scoters, 159
  baldpates, 144
  Barrows goldeneyes, 159
  black, 144, 145
  buffleheads, 159
  canvasbacks, 159, 160
  diving, 145, 156–59
  dogs for hunting, 53, 146, 149–52,
    154, 160–61
  fulvous tree, 144
  gadwalls, 144
  guns for hunting, 38, 152–54, 161
  how to cook, 153–54
  how to hunt, 145–51, 156–59
  how to identify, 144–45, 159–60
  king eiders, 159
  mallards, 38, 53, 144, 145, 147,
    162, 164
  mergansers, 159, 160
  northern eiders, 159
  old squaws, 159
  Pacific eiders, 159
  pintails, 144, 145
  puddle, 143–57, 159, 160

redhead, 159, 160
ring–necked, 157, 159
ruddy, 159
scaup, 159
shooting distance for, 17
shovelers, 144
spectacled eiders, 159
Steller's eiders, 159
surf scoters, 159
teal, 143
where to find, 145
whitewinged scoters, 159
wood, 144, 146
Ducks Unlimited, 6, 35

Edmond, Oklahoma, 52, 62–63
Eiders, 159
"Elhew Gamemaster" (English
     pointer), 119
"Elhew Huckleberry" (English
     pointer), 40
"Elhew Jungle" (English pointer), 40
"Elhew Marksman" (English pointer), 40
"Elhew Zeus" (English pointer), 40
Emporia, Kansas, 129
English cocker spaniels, 12
     pheasant and, 42–43
English pointers, 9–10
     grouse and, 104, 107–8, 117, 135–36
     partridge and, 135–36
     pheasant and, 35, 40–41
     quail and, 35, 53, 61, 90
     woodcocks and, 117, 119
English setters, 10
     grouse and, 104, 107–8, 136
     partridge and, 136
     quail and, 61, 65, 66, 70–71, 83, 90
English springer spaniels, 12
     grouse and, 61, 104, 130, 134–35
     partridge and, 134–35, 137
     pheasant and, 31, 42–43
     quail and, 61
Exotic quail, 15, 20

Falcons, for hunting prairie chickens,
     130–32
Field & Stream, 19, 130
Field Dog Stud Book, 10
Field spaniels, 12
First-aid kit, dog, 19
Fish and Wildlife Service, U.S., 16
Fish Canyon (Arizona), 75
Flat-coated retrievers, 12
Flint Hills (Kansas), 127, 128
Flushers, described, 11–12
     pheasant and, 42–43
     quail and, 89

France, 30
Franchi shotgun, 64, 68
Frazier, Frances, 57
Free, Wade, 44–51
Fulvous tree ducks, 144

Gadwalls, 144
Gambel's quail, 73, 74, 79, 80, 82, 83,
     87, 88, 91, 93, 136
     dogs for hunting, 65, 66, 70–71
     guns for hunting, 68
     how to cook, 71
     how to hunt, 67–68, 71
     how to identify, 66–67, 71
     where to find, 65–71, 81
Gambel, William, 71, 79
Game preserves
     geese on, 163
     partridge on, 99
     pheasant on, 37
     quail on, 44–48, 62–64
Geese, 15, 17, 153
     Canada, 161–64, 168–69
     dogs for hunting, 162
     on game preserves, 163
     guns for hunting, 162
     how to cook, 105–6, 168–69
     how to hunt, 162–66
     snow, 164–66, 168–69
     specklebelly, 164, 168–69
     where to find, 162, 164
"George" (German shorthaired
     pointer), 9
Georgia, 48
German longhaired pointers, 11
     pheasant and, 41–42
     quail and, 61
German roughhaired pointers, 11
     quail and, 61
German shorthaired pointers, 9, 11
     grouse and, 107–8
     pheasant and, 41–42
     quail and, 44, 45, 61, 71, 75–77, 89
German wirehaired pointers, 11
     partridge and, 98
     pheasant and, 41–42
     quail and, 61, 71, 95
Goldeneyes, 159
Golden retrievers, 12
     ducks and, 152, 161
Gould, Mike, 85, 98, 107–11
Grand Junction, Tennessee, 53
Great Lakes, 28
Griffons, wirehaired pointing, 11
     pheasant and, 41–42
     quail and, 61, 89–90, 95

Grouse, 15, 20
  blue, 104, 107–12
  dogs for hunting, 61, 103–5, 107–8,
    111, 114, 119, 130–36, 139
  pinnated (prairie chicken), 90,
    127–34, 138
  guns for hunting, 105, 110, 115,
    129, 140
  how to cook, 105–6, 111–12, 119, 133,
    140, 142
  how to hunt, 104–5, 107–11, 114–15,
    117, 128–33, 136, 139–40
  how to identify, 102, 111, 115,
    127–28, 138
  ruffed, 15, 61, 89, 100, 113–15, 117,
    119–20
  sage, 26, 101–6, 108, 111
  sharptail, 134–36, 138–40, 142
  shooting distance for, 129–30, 140
  where to find, 101, 103–5, 109–11,
    113–15, 119–20, 127–29, 134, 136,
    138–40
Guns
  described, in general, 14–18
  for doves, 126
  for ducks, 38, 152–54, 161
  for geese, 162
  for grouse, 105, 110, 115, 129, 140
  for partridge, 97–98, 140
  for pheasant, 37–38
  for quail, 64, 68, 76, 78, 79, 82, 83,
    89, 93
  for woodcocks, 118
Guns Illustrated, 37
Gyp (hunter), 9

Hartael, Harold, 155
Henderson, New York, 40
Hoisington, Kansas, 161–62
Hoisington Gun Club, 155
Hume, Edgar E., 78
Hungarian partridge, 15, 20
  dogs for hunting, 134–37
  guns for hunting, 140
  how to cook, 140, 142
  how to hunt, 136, 137, 139
  how to identify, 136
  shooting distance for, 140
  where to find, 134, 136, 138, 140
Hunting Retriever Clubs in America,
  130

Idaho, 88, 95, 98, 99, 105
International Decoy Championship, 5
International Endurance Champion-
  ship, 61

International Gun Dog Endurance
  Championship, 11
Iowa, 5, 28
Irish setters, 10
Irish water spaniels, 12
Ithaca pump shotgun, 76

Jackets, 23
"Jet" (Labrador retriever), 47

Kansas, 6, 33–34, 46, 118, 127–29, 133,
  155, 159, 161–62
"Keg of Black Powder" (Labrador
  retriever), 33–34, 130
King eiders, 159
King ranch (Texas), 54
Koelpin, Bill, 152
Korea, 30

Labrador retrievers, 6, 12, 47
  ducks and, 152, 161
  grouse and, 104, 107–8, 130
  partridge and, 98
  pheasant and, 33–34, 38, 40
  quail and, 89, 95
Lake Erie, 158
Lake Michigan, 147
Leashes, dog, 19, 61
Lilly, Ben, 81
Llewellyn setters, 65, 66, 70–71, 83
Loire River, 30
Louisiana, 158

Maine, 28, 55
Mallard Gun Club, 155
Mallards, 38, 53, 144, 145, 147,
  162, 164
Maryland, 75
Mearns, Edgar A., 71, 78–79
Mearns quail, 66, 71, 80, 94, 113
  dogs for hunting, 74–77
  guns for hunting, 76, 78
  how to cook, 79
  how to hunt, 76–79
  how to identify, 75, 79
  where to find, 72–79, 81
Memories of an Arizona Judge (Sloan), 69
Mergansers, 159, 160
Mexico, 55, 72, 74, 78, 80, 88, 95, 99,
  121, 169–70
Michigan, 127, 136, 138
Michigan Duck Hunter's Tournament, 5
Midway, Alabama, 40
Minnesota, 127
Mississippi, 48
Mississippi River, 158

Missouri, 6
Montana, 99, 105
Mountain quail
  dogs for hunting, 95
  guns for hunting, 93
  how to cook, 95
  how to hunt, 91–93, 95
  how to identify, 91, 93–94
  where to find, 91–95
Mulvane, Kansas, 33–34
Munsterlander pointers, 61

National Amateur Pheasant Champion-
  ship, 40
National Bird Dog Championship, 53,
  55–56
National Open Pheasant Shooting Dog
  Championship, 40
National Open Retriever Classic, 53
Nebraska, 127
Neckerchiefs, 23–24
Ness, Tom, 134–35
Nevada, 88, 95, 99, 105
New England, 113, 115, 118
New Hampshire, 55
New Jersey, 28
New Mexico, 28, 52, 71, 74, 80–82,
  99, 109
New Orleans, Louisiana, 158
New York, 40, 55
Nilo Plantation, 48, 57
North American Woodcock Champion-
  ship, 119
North Dakota, 105, 127, 134, 138–40
Northeast Grouse Championship, 119
Northern eiders, 159

Ocean City, Maryland, 75
O'Connor, Jack, 69
Oklahoma, 44–48, 52, 62–63, 127, 131
Old squaws, 159
Olin, John, 48–49, 57
Opie, Dan, 101
Oracle, Arizona, 65, 100
Oracle Junction, Arizona, 82
Oregon, 27–28, 55, 92, 95, 99, 101, 105,
  136, 138
Orleans, France, 30
*Ornithologists of the United States Army
  Medical Corps* (Hume), 78

Pacific eiders, 159
Pamlico Sound, 158
Pants, 24
Parton, Bill, 65–71, 82–86, 91–93,
  100, 169

Partridge
  boots for hunting, 24
  chukar, 24, 92, 96–100, 136
  dogs for hunting, 97, 98, 134–37
  on game preserves, 99
  guns for hunting, 97–98, 140
  how to cook, 100, 140, 142
  how to hunt, 96–98, 100, 136,
    137, 139
  how to identify, 100, 136
  Hungarian, 15, 20, 134–40, 142
  shooting distance for, 140
  where to find, 96, 98, 99, 134, 136,
    138, 140
Patagonia, Arizona, 77–78
Pettijohn, Gloria, 153–54
Pettijohn, Jim, 75–79, 153–54
Pheasant, 99, 105, 113, 136, 151
  boots for hunting, 24
  conservation of, 35
  dogs for hunting, 31, 33–35, 38,
    40–43, 53
  on game preserves, 37
  guns for hunting, 37–38, 64
  how to cook, 26–27
  how to hunt, 31, 33, 43
  how to identify, 28–29
  ring-necked (China bird), 7, 26–31,
    33–38, 40–43
  where to find, 20, 27–30, 33–34,
    36–37
Pheasants Forever, 6, 35
Phoenix, Arizona, 126
Pierce, B. J., 82
Pierce, John, 82
Pigeons
  dogs for hunting, 123–25
  how to hunt, 123
  how to identify, 121
  where to find, 121, 123
Pinnated grouse. *See* Prairie chickens
Pintails, 144, 145
Platte River, 147
Pointers
  described, 9–11
  ducks and, 53
  English, 9–10, 35, 40–41, 53, 61, 90,
    104, 107–8, 117, 119, 135–36
  German longhaired, 11, 41–42, 61
  German roughhaired, 11, 61
  German shorthaired, 9, 11, 41–42, 44,
    45, 61, 75, 89, 107–8
  German wirehaired, 11, 41–42, 61,
    95, 98
  grouse and, 103–4, 107–8, 117, 130,
    132, 135–36

Munsterlander, 61
  partridge and, 97, 98, 135–36
  pheasant and, 35, 40–42, 53
  pudel-, 11, 41–42, 61, 90, 95
  quail and, 35, 44, 52, 53, 61, 75–77,
    85, 89–90, 95
  wirehaired pointing griffons, 11,
    41–42, 61, 89–90, 95
  woodcocks and, 117, 119
Prairie chickens (pinnated grouse), 90,
    134, 138
  dogs for hunting, 130–33
  falcons for hunting, 130–32
  guns for hunting, 129
  how to cook, 133
  how to hunt, 128–33
  how to identify, 127–28
  shooting distance for, 129–30
  where to find, 127–29
Puddle ducks, 143, 156, 157, 159, 160
  dogs for hunting, 146, 149–52
  guns for hunting, 152–53
  how to hunt, 145–51
  how to identify, 144–45
  where to find, 145
Pudelpointers, 11
  pheasant and, 41–42
  quail and, 61, 90, 95

Quail, 103, 151, 169
  bobwhite, 17, 20, 31, 44–64, 68, 71,
    73–75, 79, 81, 87, 93, 99, 100, 104,
    111, 113, 118, 119, 121, 134, 136,
    137, 139
  boots for hunting, 24
  California, 87–90, 94
  dogs for hunting, 35, 44, 45, 52–54,
    57–63, 65, 66, 70–71, 74–77, 79, 83,
    89–90, 95
  exotic, 15, 20
  Gambel's, 65–71, 73, 74, 79–83, 87,
    88, 91, 93, 136
  on game preserves, 44–48, 62–64
  guns for hunting, 64, 68, 76, 78, 79,
    82, 83, 89, 93
  how to cook, 55–57, 71, 79, 86, 89, 95
  how to hunt, 57–64, 67–68, 71, 76–79,
    82–84, 89, 91–93, 95
  how to identify, 53–55, 66–67, 71, 75,
    79, 80, 87, 91, 93–94
  Mearns, 66, 71–81, 94, 113
  mountain, 91–95
  scaled, 24, 73, 80–86
  shooting distance for, 17, 129
  where to find, 44–55, 57, 62–64,
    72–85, 87–88, 91–95

Quail Hills Plantation, 48
Quail Unlimited, 6, 35

Rattlesnakes, weather and, 125–26
Redhead ducks, 159, 160
Red setters, 10, 61
Remington shotguns, 64
  Model 1100, 37, 82, 89, 152
Retrievers
  Chesapeake Bay, 12, 83, 152, 160–61
  curly-coated, 12
  described, 12–14
  doves and, 123–25
  ducks and, 53, 149–52, 160–61
  flat-coated, 12
  golden, 12, 152, 161
  grouse and, 104, 107–8, 130
  Labrador, 6, 12, 33, 38, 40, 47, 89, 95,
    98, 104, 107–8, 130, 152, 161
  partridge and, 98
  pheasant and, 31, 33–34, 38, 40, 53
  quail and, 53, 61–62, 89, 95
Ring-necked ducks, 157, 159
Ring-necked pheasant (China birds), 7
  conservation of, 35
  dogs for hunting, 31, 33–35
  guns for hunting, 37–38
  how to cook, 26–27
  how to hunt, 31, 33, 43
  how to identify, 28–29
  where to find, 27–30, 33–34, 36–37
Roosevelt, Theodore, 78
Ruddy ducks, 159
Ruffed grouse, 15, 89, 100
  dogs for hunting, 61, 114, 115, 117
  guns for hunting, 115
  how to cook, 119
  how to hunt, 114–15, 117
  how to identify, 115
  where to find, 113–15, 119–20
Ruffed Grouse Society, The, 35
Rutherford-Stuyvesant estate
    (New Jersey), 28

Sage grouse, 26, 108, 111
  dogs for hunting, 103–5
  guns for hunting, 105
  how to cook, 105–6
  how to hunt, 104–5
  how to identify, 102
  where to find, 101, 103–5
St. Louis, Missouri, 6
Salt River, 159
San Francisco River, 81
San Quintan, Mexico, 169

Scaled quail, 73
  boots for hunting, 24
  dogs for hunting, 83–85
  guns for hunting, 82, 83
  how to cook, 86
  how to hunt, 82–85
  how to identify, 80
  where to find, 80–85
Scaup, 159
Scoters, 159
Scottsdale, Arizona, 78
Sea of Cortez, 169
Sedona, Arizona, 65
Sequim, Washington, 130
Setters
  described, 9–10
  English, 10, 61, 65, 66, 70–71, 83, 90,
    104, 107–8, 136
  grouse and, 104, 107–8, 136
  Irish, 10
  Llewellyn, 65, 66, 70–71, 83
  partridge and, 136
  quail and, 61, 65, 66, 70–71, 83,
    85, 90
  red, 10, 61
  woodcocks and, 119
"Shadow" (German shorthaired pointer),
    75–77
Sharptail grouse
  dogs for hunting, 134–36, 139
  guns for hunting, 140
  how to cook, 140, 142
  how to hunt, 136, 139–40
  how to identify, 138
  shooting distance for, 140
  where to find, 134, 136, 138–40
"Sheila" (English springer spaniel),
    134–35
Sherrod, Steve, 131–32
Shovelers, 144
Sloan, Richard E., 69
Smith, Delmar, 52
Smith, Rick, 62–63
Smithsonian Institution, 79
Snake River, 98
Snow geese, 164–66, 168–69
Sonoita, Arizona, 77
South Dakota, 99, 105, 109, 127, 139
Specklebelly geese, 164, 168–69
Spectacled eiders, 159
Spinonis, 61
Springer spaniels
  English, 12, 31, 42–43, 61, 104, 130,
    134–35, 137
  grouse and, 61, 104, 130, 134–35
  partridge and, 134–35, 137

  pheasant and, 31, 42–43
  quail and, 61
  Welsh, 12
Springerville, Arizona, 81
Steller's eiders, 159
Stuttgart, Arkansas, 5, 159
"Super Scooper of Vondalia" (Labrador
    retriever), 6
Surf scoters, 159
Sussex spaniels, 12
Sutton Avian Research Center, 131
Sweat shirts, button-up, 23

Tags, dog, 18
Teal, 143
Tennessee, 53
Texas, 54, 55, 74, 81, 127, 164
Thunderer whistle, 60
Toenail clippers, dog, 19
Topeka, Kansas, 127
Trackers/beepers, electronic dog, 20, 22,
    58, 117

Utah, 99, 105, 109

Vermont, 55
Vests, down, 23
Vizslas, 11, 61, 90

Ward Brothers Foundation World
    Championship, 75
Washington, 55, 88, 95, 99, 105,
    130, 136
Water spaniels
  American, 12, 152
  Irish, 12
Wauwatosa, Wisconsin, 152
Weather
  dogs and, 123–25
  doves and, 123–25
  geese and, 164
  grouse and, 119–20, 139–40
  quail and, 58
  rattlesnakes and, 125–26
  wind, 43, 58, 96–97, 149, 164
  woodcocks and, 120
"Web" (Labrador retriever), 107
Wehle, Bob, 40–41, 117
Weimeraners, 11, 61, 90
Welsh springer spaniels, 12
Whistle, training, 60
Whitewinged scoters, 159
Wichita, Kansas, 33
Willamette Valley (Oregon), 28, 136
Willis, M. Wayne, 145

Winchester Arms, 57
    Model 12 shotgun, 38, 64, 129, 153
    30-40 rifle, 78
Wire cutters, 20
Wirehaired pointers
    German, 11, 41–42, 61, 95, 98
    griffons, 11, 41–42, 61, 89–90, 95
    partridge and, 98
    pheasant and, 41–42
    quail and, 61, 71, 89–90, 95
Woodcocks, 15, 117
    dogs for hunting, 117, 118

guns for hunting, 118
how to cook, 119
how to hunt, 118
how to identify, 118
where to find, 118, 120
Wood ducks, 144, 146
World Duck Calling Contest, 5
Wyoming, 105, 109

Yellville, Arkansas, 63–64
Yukon territory, Canada, 109